Modern Peacemakers

Mother Teresa

Caring for the World's Poor

MODERN PEACEMAKERS

Modern Peacemakers

Mother Teresa

Caring for the World's Poor

Louise Chipley Slavicek

CHELSEA HOUSE
PUBLISHERS
An imprint of Infobase Publishing

Mother Teresa

Copyright © 2007 by Infobase Publishing

All rights reserved. No part of this book may be reproduced or utilized in any form
or by any means, electronic or mechanical, including photocopying, recording, or by
any information storage or retrieval systems, without permission in writing from the
publisher. For information, contact:

Chelsea House
An imprint of Infobase Publishing
132 West 31st Street
New York NY 10001

ISBN-10: 0-7910-9433-2
ISBN-13: 978-0-7910-9433-4

Library of Congress Cataloging-in-Publication Data
Slavicek, Louise Chipley, 1956–
    Mother Teresa : caring for the world's poor / Louise Chipley Slavicek.
        p.   cm. — (Modern Peacemakers)
    Includes bibliographical references and index.
    ISBN 0-7910-9433-2 (hardcover)
    1. Teresea, Mother, 1910–1997. 2. Missionaries of Charity—Biography. 3. Nuns—
India—Biography. I. Title. II. Series.
    BX4406.5.Z8S59 2007
    271'.97—dc22
    [B]   2006028383

Chelsea House books are available at special discounts when purchased in bulk
quantities for businesses, associations, institutions, or sales promotions. Please call
our Special Sales Department in New York at (212) 967-8800 or (800) 322-8755.

You can find Chelsea House on the World Wide Web at http://www.chelseahouse.com.

Text design by Annie O'Donnell
Cover design by Takeshi Takahashi

Printed in the United States of America

Bang FOF 10 9 8 7 6 5 4 3 2 1

This book is printed on acid-free paper.

All links and Web addresses were checked and verified to be correct at the time of
publication. Because of the dynamic nature of the Web, some addresses and links may
have changed since publication and may no longer be valid.

TABLE OF CONTENTS

CHAPTER 1

"The Saint of the Gutters"

On a rainy Saturday afternoon in September 1997, thousands of mourners—rich and poor, Hindus, Muslims, and Christians alike—lined the streets of Calcutta to watch the city's most famous resident—Mother Teresa—come home for the last time. As a mark of the esteem in which it held the tiny nun, the Indian government had given Mother Teresa its highest honor: a state funeral. All over the nation, flags flew at half-mast, and in Calcutta a three-hour-long Mass was held in the city's gigantic Netaji Indoor Stadium. This service, for the woman popularly known as the Saint of the Gutters, was attended by presidents, prime ministers, queens, and about 15,000 other guests from around the world.

After the Mass, the funeral procession slowly wound its way through many of the same streets where Mother Teresa had once ministered to the homeless and hungry, finally ending at Acharya Jagdish Chandra Bose Road and the Missionaries of Charity mother house. There, at the headquarters of the religious order she had founded nearly a half century earlier, the 87-year-old missionary

Mother Teresa, shown above in this photograph from 1980, was famous for her missions of charity for the poor and disenfranchised in India and around the globe.

and humanitarian received a private burial, while the crowd that had gathered outside prayed and wept. As Mother Teresa's coffin was placed in the crypt, military honor guards fired a 21-gun salute—an odd tribute for the Nobel Peace Prize laureate, who objected to war and violence in any form.

Mother Teresa was born in Eastern Europe to Albanian parents, shortly before the outbreak of World War I. She first came to India as a missionary nun with the Catholic Loreto Order, when she was still a teenager. For nearly two decades, she lived a secluded and relatively comfortable life, teaching geography to middle- and upper-class Indian girls in the vast Loreto compound in Calcutta. On her few forays out of the gated complex, Teresa was stunned by the desperate poverty in the squalid neighborhoods that lay just beyond the convent walls.

In 1946, while traveling to the Loreto convent in Darjeeling, India, Mother Teresa's life changed forever. She heard God calling her to work and live among the destitute and forgotten men, women, and children who inhabited Calcutta's teeming slums. It took nearly two years for Mother Teresa to secure the Catholic Church's permission to abandon her cloistered lifestyle as a Loreto Sister and begin her mission of mercy in the streets of India's most populated city. In 1950, the Vatican officially recognized the small band of women—many of them former pupils—who had gathered around Mother Teresa as a new order: the Missionaries of Charity. For the next 47 years, Mother Teresa, assisted by her sari-clad Sisters, founded scores of schools, medical dispensaries, orphanages, and homes for the dying. They worked first in Calcutta, then throughout India, and by the late 1960s, in cities and towns all over the world. In the process, Mother Teresa became an international celebrity, a symbol of compassion and hope for people of all religious and ethnic backgrounds.

In recognition of her tireless efforts on behalf of the world's needy and unwanted, Mother Teresa received numerous honors during her lifetime, none as prestigious as the Nobel Peace Prize, granted by the Norwegian Nobel Committee in 1979. It may seem

History of the Nobel Peace Prize

The most famous and prestigious peace prize in the world, the Nobel Peace Prize, was named for Swedish chemist, engineer, and inventor Alfred B. Nobel. Born in Stockholm in 1833, Nobel's claim to fame was his invention of the powerful but relatively safe explosive, dynamite.

Upon his death in December 1896, Alfred Nobel bequeathed the vast bulk of his fortune to the establishment of the Nobel Foundation. The foundation would be responsible for awarding annual prizes to individuals or organizations whose endeavors during the past year had most benefited humanity. The prizes, each of which came with a substantial cash award, were to be granted in five areas: literature, chemistry, physics, physiology or medicine, and peace. (In 1969, a sixth prize, for economics, financed by the Swedish National Bank, was added.)

All of the prizes, with the exception of the peace prize, were to be granted by Swedish committees. In his will, Nobel directed that the peace prize be awarded by a five-person committee appointed by the Norwegian *Storting*, or Parliament. No one knows for sure why Nobel assigned responsibility for granting the peace prize to a Norwegian rather than a Swedish committee. The inventor may have been influenced by the fact that the government of Norway, which at the time of his death was in a union with Sweden under a common king, had a reputation for supporting nonviolent solutions to international disagreements. Although Nobel never stipulated that the members of the committee be Norwegian nationals, to date all committee members have been.

According to Nobel's will, the prize for peace was to be given to that person or group who "shall have done the most or the best work for fraternity between nations, for the abolition or reduction of standing armies and for the holding of peace congresses." In contrast to the other Nobel prizes, the Peace Prize may be granted to individuals or organizations that are still in the process of resolving a problem rather than solely upon the resolution of that problem.

The awarding of the Nobel Peace Prize on December 10 (the anniversary of Nobel's death in 1896) is the result of a lengthy

process. Nominations must be turned in to the Norwegian Nobel committee by February 1 of each year. Only certain individuals may nominate candidates for the prize, including current and past members of the committee, international judges, members of national governments and assemblies, Nobel Peace Prize laureates, and university professors of history, philosophy, political science, and law. The committee might receive as many as 200 nominations in a single year. After the committee creates a "short list" of nominees, the candidates are reviewed by permanent advisers as well as advisers specially appointed for their knowledge of particular nominees. Around October 1, the Peace Prize winner or winners are selected through a majority vote. The new laureate's name is usually announced in Oslo soon after that.

The first Nobel Peace Prizes were granted in 1901, five years after Alfred Nobel's death. Up to three Nobel Peace Prize laureates may be selected in a single year, and in 1901 two men shared the honor and the award money that went with it. One was Frédéric Passy of France, the founder and president of the first French peace society and chief organizer of the Universal Peace Congress, an international body dedicated to promoting peace. The other was Jean Henry Dunant of Switzerland, the founder of the Red Cross and the guiding light behind the Geneva Convention, a series of international agreements establishing rules for nations at war, including treatment of civilians, prisoners of war, the wounded, and the sick.

The many outstanding individuals selected by the Nobel committee to receive the Peace Prize since 1901 include U.S. presidents Woodrow Wilson and Jimmy Carter, German humanist and missionary doctor Albert Schweitzer, African-American civil rights activist Martin Luther King Jr., and Russian human rights advocate Andrei Sakharov. The twentieth century's most celebrated advocate of nonviolence, Mohandas Gandhi (1869–1948), was nominated five times for the prize but never received it. Many attribute this oversight to racial prejudice.

Hilary Rodham Clinton (left), at the time the First Lady of the United States, bows her head as Indian soldiers carry Mother Teresa's casket into the Netaji Indoor Stadium in Calcutta.

surprising that someone who had no formal involvement in politics or diplomacy should have been chosen for this distinguished award. The Norwegian Nobel committee, however, has a long tradition of honoring those who strive to overcome poverty, hunger, and social injustice in the world, all of which they view as grave threats to peace, both within and among nations.

Today, a decade after Mother Teresa's death, the order she founded remains as dedicated as ever to advancing the cause of world peace through works of compassion and love. From India to Italy, San Francisco to Santiago, the Sisters of the Missionaries of Charity continue Mother Teresa's selfless commitment to serve the world's suffering and forsaken and to uphold the dignity and value of all people.

CHAPTER 2

Growing Up in a Divided Land

T he woman who came to be known as Mother Teresa was born
Agnes Gonxha Bojaxhiu on August 26, 1910, in the town of
Skopje, in southeastern Europe's Balkan Peninsula. Today,
Skopje is the capital of the Republic of Macedonia, but in 1910, the
town was part of Turkey's far-ranging—and rapidly disintegrating—
Ottoman Empire. Agnes; her older brother, Lazar; her sister, Age (or
Aga); and their parents, Nikola and Drana Bojaxhiu, were ethnic
Albanians and Roman Catholic Christians, and they were in the
minority in Skopje. At the turn of the twentieth century, the city's
inhabitants were chiefly Eastern Orthodox Christians of Serbian
descent. The Bojaxhius' status as a double minority in their ethni-
cally and religiously divided hometown would have a profound
effect on young Agnes during her early years.

TUMULTUOUS TIMES FOR ALBANIANS

The year of Agnes Bojaxhiu's birth was a tumultuous one for
Albanian people on the Balkan Peninsula. Ever since their western

Balkan kingdom fell to the Ottomans in the fifteenth century, ethnic Albanians dreamed of rebuilding an independent Albania. Albanians trace their roots back to the ancient Illyrians, who once inhabited the present-day Republic of Albania. They also lived in much of the former Ottoman *vilayet* ("province") of Kosova, to the Republic's east, an area currently divided between Serbia and Macedonia. Encouraged by the steady weakening of the once-mighty Ottoman Empire during the late nineteenth and early twentieth centuries, Albanian nationalists staged their first major uprising against their longtime rulers in March 1910.

Centered in Kosova, the uprising of 1910 erupted in the town of Pristina. Soon the rebellion had spread throughout the *vilayet* (or province), where ethnic Albanians were in the majority, with the exception of a few isolated areas, such as the Bojaxhius' hometown of Skopje. By the end of the summer, an Ottoman force of 20,000 troops had managed to quell the uprising. The Ottomans suppressed the revolt with excessive brutality: They burned down entire villages and conducted public whippings of rebel leaders, which served to strengthen the resolve of the Albanian freedom fighters.

By 1912, Albanians found themselves confronting a dangerous new opponent in their ongoing quest for a state of their own. As the Ottoman Empire continued to weaken during the years leading up to World War I (1914–1918), other Balkan nations sought to grab Turkey's European possessions for themselves. Hungry for more territory and for access to the Adriatic Sea, Serbia was especially interested in acquiring Kosova and northern Albania. In the summer of 1912, Serbian troops and their Balkan allies invaded Kosova, pillaging and plundering dozens of Albanian towns and villages as they pushed southward.

Within a few months, Serbian forces occupied most of the vilayet and were close to expelling the Ottomans from the Balkan Peninsula. Worried that their Slavic neighbor to the south was becoming too powerful, the leaders of the Austrian-Hungarian

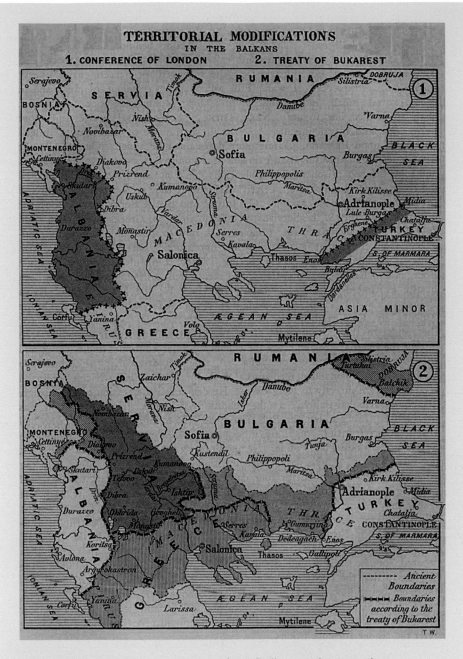

This map shows the boundaries of the Balkan nations as they appeared before World War I. Mother Teresa's birthplace, Skopje, is labeled as "Uskub," the Turkish name for the Macedonian town.

Empire sought to prevent Serbia from annexing all of Albania. To that end, in November 1912, Austria-Hungary and the other "Great Powers" of Europe, including France, Great Britain, and Germany, formally backed the creation of an independent Albanian state along the Adriatic coastline.

ETHNIC VIOLENCE IN KOSOVA

Albanians throughout the Balkans were elated at the formation of the new Albanian state. In Kosova, however, the rejoicing was soon replaced by terror, as the occupying Serbian troops turned viciously on the province's Albanian residents. While the leaders of the Great Powers debated the future of Kosova among themselves, Serbian atrocities against Albanian Kosovars increased, and thousands of men, women, and children were slaughtered.

According to some, the escalating violence in Kosova was motivated by more than ethnic and religious prejudice: The killings were also spurred by a desire to decimate the province's Albanian population. Rumor had it that the Great Powers intended to give the new Albanian state those portions of Kosova in which ethnic Albanians held a substantial majority, and Serbian leaders were grimly determined to hold onto as much of the former vilayet as possible. "The [Serbian] massacres are taking place for statistical purposes," a British diplomat in Kosova alleged in 1913. "I am beginning to suspect that much of the Albanian population is being murdered in cold blood."[1]

Horrific stories of Serbian barbarity against Albanian Kosovars soon began to trickle out of the beleaguered province. In Pristina, 5,000 ethnic Albanians were allegedly roped together and mowed down by Serbian machine-gun fire on a single day in late 1912. Agnes's hometown of Skopje was also the site of numerous purported atrocities. According to some eyewitness accounts, Serbian troops raped, tortured, or murdered hundreds of the town's Albanian residents, slaughtering even infants and young children.

A PROSPEROUS AND CLOSE-KNIT FAMILY

The Bojaxhius had to have been generally aware of the ethnic violence in Skopje and Kosova during the years leading up to World War I. The precise impact of the turmoil on young Agnes and her family, however, like so many details of Mother Teresa's early life, is shrouded in mystery. Over the years, Mother Teresa consistently refused to discuss her childhood or family in any detail. Her personal life, she insisted, was of no importance. What really mattered was her missionary and charitable work, and that was all she wanted to talk about.

What little information biographers have been able to gather about Mother Teresa's early childhood indicates that her family was financially comfortable and close knit. Her father, Nikola Bojaxhiu, was a successful investor, building contractor, and international merchant, who spoke four languages in addition to his native Albanian. He owned several valuable properties in the Skopje area. Surrounded by fruit trees and flower gardens, the house that he, his wife, and their three children lived in was elegant and spacious; it even included separate guest quarters.

Nikola Bojaxhiu, or Kole, as he was generally known, was not only an excellent provider but also an affectionate and attentive father and husband. He was frequently away from Skopje on business, and whenever he was expected home, his family was filled with joyful anticipation, Lazar Bojaxhiu recalled. Decades later, Lazar still remembered fondly how his father could always be counted on to bring back small gifts for his wife and each of the children and to entertain them with exciting and often humorous accounts of his travels.

HER MOTHER'S DAUGHTER

Drana Bojaxhiu, although devoted to her husband, was decidedly more serious than her sociable and fun-loving husband. One of the few stories Mother Teresa ever related about her early childhood highlights her mother's no-nonsense style and disdain for waste of any sort—character traits that the famous missionary herself would display throughout her adult life. One evening, when their father was out of town on a business trip, Teresa recalled, the Bojaxhiu children lingered at the dinner table, swapping jokes and silly stories. Their mother listened for a while, then quietly left the room. Suddenly the entire house was plunged into darkness: Drana Bojaxhiu had shut off the main power switch. "She told us that there was no use wasting electricity so that such foolishness could go on," Mother Teresa explained to a biographer.[2]

According to Lazar Bojaxhiu, it was clear from the time she was very young that Agnes, much more than either of her two siblings, was her mother's child. Agnes was not only naturally obedient but also unusually serious for her age, he remembered. For instance, whenever young Lazar gave in to temptation and stole jam from the pantry, Agnes could be counted on to give her older brother a stern lecture. To his relief, however, she never told their parents what had happened.

Lazar Bojaxhiu also remembered that his younger sister instructed him about the importance of treating persons of authority—and especially church officials—with respect. During Agnes's early childhood, the priest at the Church of the Sacred Heart, the local Catholic parish, was a severe disciplinarian, with rigid ideas regarding how children should behave. Young Lazar and his friends heartily disliked the ill-tempered priest and often complained about him behind his back. When Lazar criticized the cleric in front of Agnes, however, she was dismayed and did not hesitate to express her disapproval to her older sibling: "It is your duty to love him and give him respect," she scolded. "He is Christ's priest."[3]

TRAGEDY STRIKES THE BOJAXHIU FAMILY

Shortly before Agnes turned four years old, World War I erupted in Europe, pitting the Allies—Serbia, Russia, France, Belgium, and Great Britain—against the Central Powers of Austria-Hungary,

Germany, Turkey, and Bulgaria. Throughout most of the more than four-year-long conflict, Kosova was occupied by Bulgarian and Austrian troops, bringing a halt to Serbian atrocities against the province's Albanian population. Following the Allied victory in November 1918, the authors of the Treaty of Versailles took it upon themselves to redraw the map of southeastern Europe. According to the terms of the peace treaty, the Bojaxhius' hometown and province were annexed to the newly created Kingdom of the Serbs, Croats, and Slovenes known from 1929 until 1992 as Yugoslavia. In 1992, Yugoslavia became the independent republics of Slovenia, Macedonia, Montenegro, and Bosnia.

Governed from the city of Belgrade on the Danube River, this new kingdom was overwhelmingly Slavic; ethnic Albanians like Agnes and her family made up only a small fraction of the country's 12 million inhabitants. Within the province of Kosova, however, Albanians still remained the single largest ethnic group. Consequently, many Albanian Kosovars believed that their region should be allowed to leave the new federation created by the Versailles Treaty, to become part of what they referred to as a "Greater Albania."

Kole Bojaxhiu was a passionate supporter of Albanian inde-pendence. After World War I, he became heavily involved in the movement for a Greater Albania. His devotion to the cause was so strong that, in 1919, he traveled more than 150 miles northward to Belgrade to attend a political gathering for Albanian Kosovars who wanted their region to be incorporated into Albania. To his family's horror, late one evening, a few days after Kole had set off for the Yugoslavian capital, the previously healthy 45-year-old returned home in the carriage of the local Italian consul, barely conscious and obviously on the brink of death. Determined that her husband should receive the last rites of the Catholic Church before he died, Drana ordered nine-year-old Agnes to fetch the parish priest as quickly as possible.

When she could not track down the local priest at the church or rectory, Agnes decided to go to the Skopje railway station. Apparently, someone told her that a Catholic cleric who was passing through the area had just been spotted there. Rushing to the station, Agnes persuaded the unkown priest to come home with her, where he administered the last rites to Kole and prayed with the frightened family. Forty-eight hours later, Kole was dead. Even today, the cause of his illness and rapid demise remains a mystery. Many years after the tragedy, however, Lazar Bojaxhiu revealed to an interviewer that he blamed the Yugoslavian government for his father's untimely death. Government agents had secretly poisoned Kole while he was attending a political dinner in Belgrade, Lazar theorized, because of his father's involvement in the campaign to take Kosova away from Yugoslavia.

DRANA RISES TO THE OCCASION

Drana Bojaxhiu was devastated by the sudden loss of her husband. In her grief, she withdrew from her family, relying on 15-year-old Age to run the household and watch the younger children for her. Drana's despair only grew when her husband's former business partner stole Kole's share of the earnings and then disappeared, leaving the Bojaxhius all but penniless.

Several months after Kole's death, however, Drana finally began to pull herself together. Realizing that she had no choice but to become the family's breadwinner, she set up a small business of her own, selling embroidered cloth and other locally crafted textiles. Soon she had expanded her business to include the hand-woven rugs for which Skopje was famous throughout the Balkans. The family would never again attain the level of prosperity they had enjoyed while Kole was alive, but thanks to Drana's initiative and hard work, they always had a roof over their heads and food on their table.

All her life, Drana had been deeply religious, but now more than ever she turned to her faith and her church to guide and sustain her. Every evening, she and the children prayed together, and most mornings they attended Catholic Mass at the nearby Church of the Sacred Heart. Drana also encouraged her children to take part in a wide range of church activities. She realized that the close-knit, predominantly Albanian parish not only provided the Bojaxhiu children with vital spiritual and emotional support, but also with a sense of cultural and religious identity in a town where they were significantly outnumbered by Slavs and Eastern Orthodox Christians. Even within the Albanian community, the Bojaxhius were in the minority: Most Albanians had abandoned Catholicism in favor of the Islamic faith of their Ottoman conquerors centuries earlier. In fact, during the early 1900s, only about 25 percent of Kosova's Albanian population was Catholic, and even less—perhaps as little as 10 percent—of the population of the nation of Albania was Catholic.

"ALL OF THEM ARE OUR PEOPLE"

The Bojaxhiu family had long been known in Skopje for their generosity toward the town's poor and downtrodden. Kole Bojaxhiu, a firm believer in the importance of Christian charity, made a point of opening his dinner table to the Bojaxhius' less fortunate neighbors. "Never eat a single mouthful unless you are sharing it with others," he often admonished his children.[4] Drana Bojaxhiu, who shared her husband's strong commitment to assisting anyone in need, regularly took food, clothing, and other items to the destitute and sick of the parish. Mother Teresa recalled that her mother never broadcast her good deeds, however: "When you do good, do it unobtrusively, as if you were tossing a pebble into the sea," Drana liked to say.[5]

After Kole's death, the Bojaxhiu home continued to be a refuge for the hungry and forgotten. Although there was far less money to spare in the household than when her husband had been alive, Drana still opened the family dinner table to anyone in need, from distant relatives to complete strangers. Years later, Lazar remembered asking his mother about the steady stream of guests who shared their meals, most of whom he had never met before. "Some of them are relations," she answered, "but all of them are our people."[6]

Throughout her high-school years, Agnes belonged to the local parish choir and the Albanian Catholic Choir of Skopje, often performing duets with her sister, Age.

Another of Agnes's favorite pastimes during her teen years was writing. She penned two articles that appeared in the local Albanian-language newspaper, *Blagovest*, during the late 1920s. Although Agnes clearly had a talent for journalistic writing, her true passion was poetry. According to biographer Eileen Eagan, "she often carried a notebook with her and on occasion would read to her friends the poetry she had written."[9]

FATHER JAMBREKOVIC AND THE CATHOLIC MISSIONS IN INDIA

Throughout her adolescence, Agnes was active in the Church of the Sacred Heart. Indeed, Lazar Bojaxhiu would later muse that the parish church was his younger sister's second home. Agnes's growing involvement in the church coincided with the arrival of Father Franjo Jambrekovic as Sacred Heart's new parish priest in 1925. A charismatic Jesuit priest with a knack for communicating with young people, Jambrekovic made it a point to reach out to his teenaged parishioners from the start. He established a branch of a society for young Catholics called the Sodality (fellowship) of the Blessed Virgin Mary at the parish, which Agnes and many of her friends enthusiastically joined. He also encouraged the teens in his flock to volunteer their time to assist others within the congregation. Agnes agreed to help provide religious instruction in Albanian to the parish's youngest children. She quickly discovered that she liked teaching and seemed to have a natural aptitude for it.

Soon after arriving at the Church of the Sacred Heart, Father Jambrekovic began to assemble a parish library designed to appeal to the congregation's younger members. Agnes, who loved books and learning, spent many happy hours in the new library. Among the various Catholic newspapers and magazines in the church collection were several missionary publications. Agnes was especially intrigued by a richly illustrated periodical entitled *Catholic Missions*. The magazine featured a number of dramatic and inspiring articles by Yugoslavian Jesuits, in which the priests recounted their missionary exploits in far-off India. "They used to give us the most beautiful descriptions about the experiences they had with the people, and especially the children in India," Mother Teresa would recall of the *Catholic Missions* articles decades later.[10]

Father Jambrekovic reinforced Agnes's growing interest in the Indian missions at the fellowship meetings he helped organize. At these gatherings, he would sometimes read aloud from letters written by his fellow Yugoslavian Jesuits in Bengal, India. His deep admiration for the missionaries' dedication and sacrifice was obvious. Jambrekovic also encouraged the young people to pray regularly for the Catholic missionaries in India and organized monetary collections within the parish to support their work.

"TO GO OUT AND GIVE THE LIFE OF CHRIST TO THE PEOPLE"

Mother Teresa later revealed that she first felt a call to enter the religious life when she was just 12 years old. She was visiting the Catholic shrine of Our Lady of Cernagore, in the mountain town of Letnice, near Skopje. By the time she graduated from high school and turned 18, Agnes Bojaxhiu had come to believe that God was not only calling her to be a nun but more specifically to be a missionary nun, "to go out and give the life of Christ to the people," as she put it.[11]

At first, Agnes was plagued by doubts as to the authenticity of her call to missionary work. A conversation with Father Jambrekovic, however, set her mind at ease. "If the thought that God may be calling you to serve him and your neighbor makes you happy, then that may be the best proof of the genuineness of your vocation," he told her. "Joy that comes from the depths of your being is like a compass by which you can tell what direction your life should follow. This is the case even when the road you must take is a difficult one."[12] Father Jambrekovic's words must have struck a chord with Agnes. Not long after their conversation, she informed her mother that she planned to apply for acceptance to the Sisters of Our Lady of Loreto, a Catholic teaching order known for its missionary work in India.

Although Agnes was convinced that her calling to be a missionary nun was indeed genuine, the decision to leave her home and family for a life of service to God was a difficult one for her. Decades later, in one of only a few references to her early years, Mother Teresa said about her family: "We were very closely united, especially after my father's death."[13] Agnes was especially

Eastern Orthodoxy Versus Roman Catholicism

For approximately the first 1,200 years of its existence, the Christian Church was officially united. Then, during the third century, the chief Christian power on Earth, the Roman Empire, split into western and eastern halves—one predominantly Latin speaking and governed from Rome and the other predominantly Greek speaking and governed from Constantinople. As a direct consequence of the splintering of the empire, Christianity began to develop distinctive western and eastern branches, each with its own ideas about theology and church practices. By the late 1200s, the steadily growing differences between the two branches of Christianity led to the creation of two separate churches: Roman Catholic and Eastern Orthodox.

Many believe that the reason for the split between eastern and western Christianity during the Middle Ages was the doctrine of papal supremacy. The western, or Roman Catholic, branch of the church contended that the bishop of Rome—the pope—was the supreme judge in matters of discipline and faith. In contrast, the eastern, or Orthodox, branch emphasized the equality of all bishops and the authority of councils, in which local churches were given an equal say.

close to her mother, whom she referred to as *Nana Loke*, meaning "mother of my soul" in Albanian.

Agnes understood that, when she left Skopje to join the Sisters of Loreto, she might very well be saying goodbye to her mother and siblings forever. During the early twentieth century, joining a missionary order involved not only the lifelong commitment to chastity that all nuns must make but "most likely also the prospect of a lifetime of total separation from blood relatives, friends and homeland," noted Kathryn Spink, one of Mother Teresa's biographers. She added, "At the time there was little opportunity for home visits, or travel by family members to distant lands."[14]

When Agnes told her mother she intended to become a missionary nun, Drana was crushed. She locked herself in her

In addition to their opposing views regarding the central authority of the pope, Eastern Orthodox Christians and Roman Catholics also hold different views on a number of theological points. For example, both the Orthodox and Roman Catholics revere Mary, the mother of Jesus, but the Orthodox do not accept the Roman Catholic doctrine of her immaculate conception, meaning that she was conceived and born without original sin. Another basic difference between the two churches is that Eastern Orthodoxy teaches that the Holy Spirit proceeds from God the Father alone, whereas Roman Catholicism contends that the Holy Spirit proceeds from both God the Father and his son, Jesus Christ.

Today, as in Mother Teresa's childhood, Eastern Orthodoxy is the chief Christian Church in the Balkans and throughout most of Eastern Europe. It is the principal religious body, not only in the Bojaxhiu family's homeland of Macedonia, but also in Serbia, Montenegro, Bulgaria, Romania, Greece, Cyprus, Russia, Georgia, Ukraine, and Belarus. The Orthodox Church, which has an estimated worldwide membership of 200 to 300 million, also maintains a scattered presence in a number of other countries, including the United States, Albania, the Czech Republic, Estonia, Finland, Latvia, Lithuania, and Poland.

bedroom and prayed for 24 hours, without stopping. When she finally emerged from her room, Drana had clearly reconciled herself to her daughter's decision. "Put your hand in [God's] hand and walk all the way with Him," she advised her youngest child.[15] Not long afterward, Agnes left Skopje to go to Ireland, the location of the mother house (main convent) of the Sisters of Loreto. Drana and Age traveled with the 18-year-old as far as Zagreb, near the Yugoslav-Austrian border, where they bid her a tearful goodbye. Agnes would never see her mother or her older sister again.

CHAPTER 3

The Sisters of Loreto

Although Drana and Age Bojaxhiu supported Agnes's decision to become a nun, Lazar Bojaxhiu was dismayed when he first heard about his younger sister's plans during the summer of 1928. Ambitious and adventurous, he had left Skopje for Albania several years earlier, after he was awarded a place in a military academy. Lazar Bojaxhiu was now a lieutenant in the Albanian royal army, and he was extremely proud of all he had accomplished. Surely, his bright and strong-minded sister could do more with her life than become a nun, he thought. Determined to set his sister straight, he wrote her a stern letter, in which he admonished her not to throw her future away on a whim. Agnes stood her ground, however. "You think you are important because you are an officer serving a king of two million subjects," she wrote back. "But I am serving the King of the whole world! Which of us do you think is in the better place?"[16]

THE IBVM AND THE SISTERS OF LORETO

The Sisters of Loreto, the religious order that 18-year-old Agnes had resolved to join, with or without her older brother's approval, was a branch of the Institute of the Blessed Virgin Mary (IBVM), one of the leading Catholic women's orders of the early twentieth century. Founded in 1609 by a 24-year-old Englishwoman named Mary Ward, the IBVM was meant to be a new sort of religious community for women, a self-governing congregation similar to the all-male Society of Jesus (Jesuits) founded by St. Ignatius Loyola more than a half century earlier.

In many respects, Mary Ward was a woman ahead of her time. In an era when females were commonly assumed to be morally and intellectually inferior to males, Ward argued that women had much to contribute and ought to be given a more influential role in the Catholic Church and society in general. In order to develop what she considered her gender's untapped abilities, Ward wanted the IBVM to provide greater educational opportunities for girls in England and throughout Europe. Although Catholic nuns traditionally dressed in restrictive religious habits and spent their lives cloistered—or enclosed—within a convent, Ward insisted that members of her order dress in everyday clothing and live within the communities they served.

In 1631, concerns over Ward's unconventional ideas and practices prompted Catholic authorities to temporarily disband the IBVM. After Ward's death in 1645, however, the order gradually made a comeback. During the eighteenth and early nineteenth centuries, a number of new girls' schools and convents opened across Europe. The revived order was considerably more conservative than in Ward's day, though; members donned traditional religious habits and resided in enclosed convents, just like other Catholic nuns.

In 1822, a devout young Irish woman by the name of Frances Ball founded her homeland's branch of the IBVM at Rathfarnham Abbey, near Dublin. The IBVM's Irish offshoot soon came to be known as the Sisters of Loreto, after a Catholic shrine in Loreto, Italy, where Mary Ward had often prayed. In response to a plea from a German missionary to India for nuns to teach there, in

1841 the Loreto Sisters expanded their educational work overseas, establishing a girls' school in Calcutta, in the province of Bengal. By January 1842, the nuns were operating six boarding and day schools for girls around the city. At first, the nuns' students were the daughters of Irish and English soldiers serving in India, which officially came under British rule in the mid-nineteenth century. Over time, though, the various Loreto schools in Bengal would begin to attract more and more native Indian students, most of them from well-off Hindu or Muslim families.

RATHFARNHAM

In early October 1928, Agnes arrived at the Loreto mother house at Rathfarnham, Ireland, the required first stop on her long journey to India. She was accompanied by Betika Kanjc, another young Catholic woman from Yugoslavia who hoped to serve as a missionary nun in India. During the teenagers' nearly two-month stay at the Loreto mother house, they would be introduced to the history and goals of the IBVM and receive intensive training in English, because all classes at the Sisters' Calcutta schools were conducted in that language.

Although Agnes did not know a single word of English when she arrived at Rathfarnham, she had apparently inherited her father's talent for languages, because she proved a quick study. Like Betika Kanjc and the other postulants (or candidates for admission to the order) when Agnes was not in class, she was usually performing some kind of manual labor around the convent or taking part in the Divine Offices. The Divine Offices are specific prayers that are supposed to be recited at certain times of the day, in accordance with church law. The prayer schedule for the Sisters of Loreto was both rigid and demanding. Eight times in every 24-hour period, bells rang to call the postulants and nuns to devotions. The first daily "prayer event" occurred several hours before sunrise and the last took place right before bedtime.

FIRST IMPRESSIONS OF INDIA

On December 1, 1928, Agnes and Betika left Ireland on the sailing ship the *Marcha*. They were headed for India. The young women's long and arduous voyage would take them through the Atlantic Ocean, the Mediterranean Sea, the Suez Canal, the Red Sea, the Arabian Sea, and the Indian Ocean, before they reached the Bay of Bengal.

After nearly a month at sea, the *Marcha* made landfall for the first time at the port of Colombo, on what is today the island of Sri Lanka. In a letter to the *Catholic Missions*—the same missionary magazine that she had enjoyed reading back in Skopje—Agnes vividly described her initial impressions of India, "the land of her dreams":

> We arrived at Colombo on 27 December. . . . We observed the life in the streets with strange feelings. It was easy to pick out the Europeans' elegant garments, among the multicolored garments of the dark-skinned people. Most of the Indians were half-naked, their skin and hair glistening in the hot sun. Clearly there was great poverty among them. The ones for whom we felt the greatest pity were the men who, like horses, dragged their own little carts along the streets.[17]

The *Marcha's* next port of call was Madras, on India's southeastern coast. There, Agnes and Betika were appalled to find even more terrible living conditions than those they had witnessed in Colombo. "We reached Madras . . . at nightfall," Agnes wrote in the *Catholic Missions*:

> Already the shore presented a sad spectacle of these poor people. When next day we visited the city, we were shocked to the depths of our beings by the indescribable poverty. Many families live in the streets. . . . Day and night they live in the open on mats they have made from large palm leaves—or, often, on the bare ground. . . . As we went along the street we came

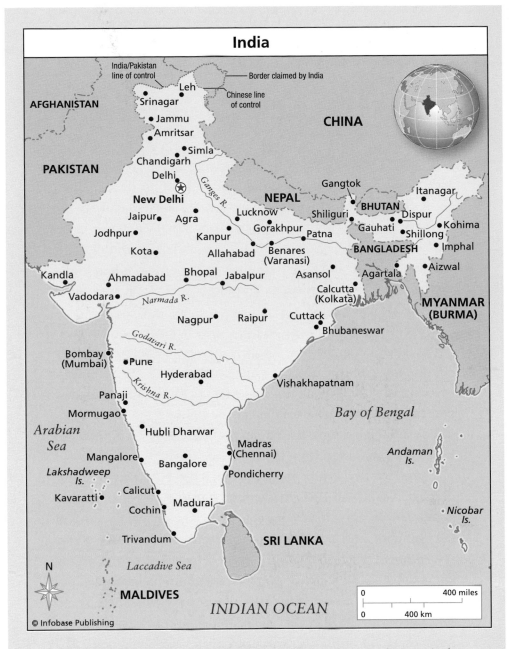

India

India/Pakistan line of control — Border claimed by India

Leh

Chinese line of control

AFGHANISTAN

Srinagar

Jammu

Amritsar

CHINA

Simla

Chandigarh

PAKISTAN

Delhi

New Delhi

Ganges R.

NEPAL

Gangtok

Itanagar

BHUTAN

Dispur

Jaipur

Agra

Lucknow

Shiliguri

Gauhati

Kohima

Jodhpur

Kanpur

Gorakhpur

Patna

Shillong

Imphal

Kota

Allahabad

Benares (Varanasi)

BANGLADESH

Kandla

Ahmadabad

Bhopal

Jabalpur

Asansol

Agartala

Aizwal

Vadodara

Narmada R.

Nagpur

Raipur

Calcutta (Kolkata)

Cuttack

MYANMAR (BURMA)

Godavari R.

Bhubaneswar

Bombay (Mumbai)

Pune

Hyderabad

Vishakhapatnam

Krishna R.

Panaji

Mormugao

Bay of Bengal

Arabian Sea

Hubli Dharwar

Andaman Is.

Mangalore

Bangalore

Madras (Chennai)

Lakshadweep Is.

Calicut

Pondicherry

Kavaratti

Cochin

Madurai

Nicobar Is.

Trivandum

SRI LANKA

N

Laccadive Sea

MALDIVES

INDIAN OCEAN

0   400 miles

0   400 km

© Infobase Publishing

The map above shows India and its cities as they are known today. In the east is Calcutta, or Kolkata, which would become Mother Teresa's home.

across one family gathered around a dead relative, wrapped in worn red rags. . . . It was a horrifying sight. If our people could only see all this, they would stop grumbling about their own misfortunes and offer up thanks to God for blessing them with such abundance.[18]

NOVICE

Following a brief stopover in Calcutta, Agnes and Betika set off up the Ganges River to Darjeeling, in the foothills of the Himalayas, where the Loreto Sisters maintained a convent and school. Darjeeling, the two young postulants soon discovered, was nothing like Colombo or Madras. The town was the playground of the wealthy, a scenic and fashionable haven for British officials and their families trying to escape the summer heat of Calcutta, some 400 miles to the south.

After about four months of instruction in prayer and the rules of the Loreto order, on May 23, 1929, Agnes and Betika officially became novices, the next stage after postulant in the process of becoming a nun. To mark this important occasion, they took new names in honor of a favorite saint. Betika became Mary Magdalene and Agnes took the name of Teresa, after St. Thérèse of Lisieux, a French nun from the Carmelite order.

Although St. Thérèse of Lisieux had only been canonized—or declared a saint—in 1925, by the time Agnes decided to take her name, Thérèse was already one of the best-known female saints of the Catholic Church. Her fame rested primarily on a slim volume she authored when she was in her early twenties. At the urging of her spiritual director, the young French nun had recorded her life story during a bout with tuberculosis, a serious lung disease. Published with the title *Story of My Soul*, one year after Thérèse's untimely death in 1897 (at age 24), the brief autobiography was a surprise bestseller.

People were particularly drawn to Thérèse's principle of "The Little Way," which involved trying to live one's life with a childlike trust in God. Even though her frail health meant that she could never be a missionary herself, two years after Thérèse's canonization, she was pronounced the patroness of foreign missions because of her deep interest in the church's missionary endeavors. Because there was already a novice at Darjeeling named Thérèse, Agnes decided to adopt the Spanish spelling of the French saint's name by dropping the "h" and the accented characters, and substituting an "a" for the final "e."

FIRST VOWS

In May 1931, Teresa graduated from her novitiate and took her first vows as a Sister of Loreto. These temporary vows of obedience, chastity, and poverty were to be renewed each year until Sister Teresa was ready to take her final vows. The vow of obedience meant that Teresa promised to follow God's will in all things; the vow of chastity required that she put her love for the Almighty above all else and remain a virgin for the rest of her life; and the vow of poverty meant that she would relinquish all private property and live as simply as possible.

Shortly after taking her first vows, Sister Teresa was assigned to teach in the Loreto convent school at Darjeeling, which served British and Indian girls. As part of her on-the-job training as a Loreto instructor, Sister Teresa taught a variety of subjects, including arithmetic, religion, and geography. She also began to study Bengali and Hindi, in order to better communicate with her Indian students.

Most of Sister Teresa's pupils at the Darjeeling school came from middle- or upper-class backgrounds. A short stint as an aide at a local medical clinic in 1931, however, placed the young nun in direct contact with India's impoverished masses. Later that year, *Catholic Missions* published a poignant report from Sister Teresa about her experiences at the Darjeeling medical station. Her letter reveals that, at age 21, Agnes Bojaxhiu had already developed the profoundly spiritual attitude toward human suffering for which she would become famous in later years:

In the hospital's pharmacy hangs a picture of the Redeemer surrounded by a throng of suffering people, on whose faces the torments of their lives have been engraved. Each morning, before I start work, I look at this picture. In it is concentrated everything that I feel. I think, 'Jesus, it is for you and for these souls!' Then I open the door. The tiny veranda is always full of the sick, the wretched and the miserable. All eyes are fixed, full of hope, on me. . . . Many have come from a distance, walking for as much as three hours. . . . Their ears and feet are covered in sores. . . . One is in the terminal stage of tuberculosis. . . . [A] man arrives with a bundle from which two dry twigs protrude. They are the legs of a child. . . . The man is afraid that we do not want to take the child, and says, "If you do not want him, I will throw him into the grass. The jackals will not turn up their noses at him." My heart freezes. The poor child! Weak, and blind—totally blind. With much pity and love I take the little one into my arms, and fold him in my apron. The child has found a second mother. "Who so receives a child, receives me," said the divine Friend of all little Ones. The incident of the blind child is the crowning point of my working day.[19]

LORETO ENTALLY

By the time Teresa's *Catholic Missions* article was published in November 1931, she had already left Darjeeling for a new work assignment and a new home. Teresa was now a resident of "Loreto Entally," her order's extensive compound in Entally, a district of Calcutta on the city's east side. The young nun spent her days teaching geography to adolescent girls at St. Mary's, a Catholic secondary school located on the convent grounds. About 200 students, virtually all of them Indian, attended St. Mary's, and classes were taught in Bengali and English. The pupils' backgrounds differed greatly: Many came from comfortable circumstances, but the school also provided free tuition and room and board to a number of impoverished and orphaned girls. Another, bigger school within the Entally compound catered primarily to young ladies from upper-class British and Indian families.

Although Loreto Entally bordered one of Calcutta's numerous slums, Moti Jheel, the compound was truly a world unto itself, providing its residents with a safe and sequestered environment. On all sides, high, thick walls surrounded the complex, and guards were posted continuously at its gated entrance. Obliged by the laws of the Loreto order to live a cloistered existence, the Sisters themselves seldom set foot out of their carefully enclosed and guarded compound. Only in case of a dire emergency or by the express order of the Mother Superior could Sister Teresa or any of her fellow nuns leave the complex.

Despite her order's strict rules of enclosure, however, Sister Teresa was not entirely divorced from the grinding poverty that surrounded Loreto Entally. During her fourth year at the compound, she was given an unprecedented opportunity to venture out of the convent and into the rough streets and alleys of Moti Jheel. In 1935, Teresa's Mother Superior assigned the young nun to spend part of each weekday teaching reading, writing, and arithmetic at Bengali Medium, a Catholic primary school located a short walk away from Loreto Entally.

The rooms at St. Mary's School were spacious and well equipped. In contrast, at Bengali Medium, Teresa had to conduct her classes in a long, narrow chapel that had been partitioned into five cramped schoolrooms, or in a converted stable, and even outside, in the school courtyard. Nonetheless, Teresa was grateful for the opportunity to offer her services where she knew they were both desperately needed and deeply appreciated. She quickly discovered that the raggedly clothed children of Bengali Medium were enthusiastic learners, and they blossomed under her loving attention and concern. Even the smallest show of approval or affection, such as placing her hand on each child's head, Sister Teresa reported, brought joy to her young charges.

FINAL VOWS AND NEW RESPONSIBILITIES

On May 14, 1937, 26-year-old Agnes Bojaxhiu took her final vows of chastity, obedience, and poverty as a Loreto Sister, in the chapel of the order's convent at Darjeeling. During the ceremony, Agnes, dressed in a long white wedding gown, was presented with a simple gold band, which symbolized her eternal commitment to her "Bridegroom," Jesus Christ. From that moment on, the newly professed nun was known as "Mother Teresa" instead of Sister Teresa, in accordance with the customs of the Loreto order.

After returning to Calcutta, Mother Teresa continued to teach geography at St. Mary's, but was relieved of her duties at Bengali Medium. Teresa no longer had time to teach outside the Loreto compound. She had been given an important new assignment: She was to replace her longtime supervisor, Mother Cenacle, as head-

"In the Missions, You Have to be Prepared for Anything"

From 1935 to 1937 Mother Teresa spent part of each school day away from the Entally compound, teaching impoverished children from nearby neighborhoods. The following is a first-person account of her experiences at St. Teresa's Primary School—otherwise known as Bengali Medium—in the eastern Calcutta slum of Moti Jheel.

When they saw me for the first time, the children wondered whether I was an evil spirit or a goddess. For them there was no middle way. Anyone who is good is adored like one of their gods; anyone who is ill-disposed is feared as though he were a demon, and kept at arm's length.

I rolled up my sleeves immediately, rearranged the whole room, found water and a broom and began to sweep the floor. This greatly astonished them. They had never seen a schoolmistress start lessons like that, particularly because in India cleaning is something that the lower castes do; and they stood staring at me for a long time. Seeing me cheerful and smiling, the girls

mistress of St. Mary's. Mother Cenacle had been in poor health and could no longer handle the demands of the position. As part of her new duties as principal of St. Mary's, Teresa was also put in charge of an order of Bengali nuns affiliated with the Loreto Sisters. The Daughters of St. Anne, as the women were known, made up most of the teaching staff at St. Mary's. They taught classes in their native tongue and dressed in saris rather than the European-style religious habits of the Loreto nuns. The traditional garment of Indian women, a sari is a long strip of silk or cotton cloth that can be draped around the body in various styles.

Shortly after her promotion, Mother Teresa sent a letter to her mother, who now resided in Tirana, Albania, with Lazar and Age. "This is my new life," she wrote cheerfully: "Our center here is very fine. I am a teacher and I love the work. I am also Head

began to help me, and the boys brought me more water. After two hours that room was at least in part transformed into a clean schoolroom. It was a long room, which had originally been a chapel and is now divided into five classes.

When I arrived there were 52 children, and now there are over 300. (I also teach in another school where there are about 200 children, but it is not so much like a school as a stable! And then again I teach in another place, in a kind of courtyard.)

When I first saw where the children slept and ate, I was full of anguish. It is not possible to find worse poverty. And yet, they are happy. Blessed childhood! Though when we first met, they were not at all joyful. They began to leap and sing only when I had put my hand on each dirty little head. From that day onwards they called me "Ma," which means "Mother." How little it takes to make simple souls happy! The mothers started bringing their children to me to bless. At first I was amazed at this request, but in the missions you have to be prepared for anything.*

*David Porter, *Mother Teresa: The Early Years*. Grand Rapids, Mich.: W.B. Eerdmans, 1986, p. 47.

of the whole school, and everybody wishes me well."[20] Although she could not have imagined it at the time, Mother Teresa's happy and tranquil "new life" at St. Mary's would soon be shattered by a succession of disturbing events.

CALCUTTA IN WARTIME

When Great Britain entered World War II on the Allied side in September 1939, the British colony of India was swept into the conflict, as well. Although Calcutta was far from the center of the fighting, the war would have devastating consequences for the city and its inhabitants.

After India's neighbor, the British colony of Burma, was over-run by Japanese troops in 1942, the British army requisitioned a number of buildings in Calcutta, including the Loreto Entally compound. The buildings were converted into a military hospital. Mother Teresa and her staff at St. Mary's School, together with about 300 boarding students, were compelled to move to Convent Road, elsewhere in Calcutta. Adding to the disruptions in the city, millions of destitute Burmese refugees poured into Calcutta in the wake of the Japanese invasion of their homeland.

Coming on the heels of the Japanese occupation of Burma and the resulting flood of refugees into Calcutta was another war-related disaster: the Great Famine of 1942–1943. Grave food shortages first began to develop in the city after the British military abruptly closed the upper regions of the Indian Ocean to supply ships. About the same time, the military took over virtually the entire Indian transportation system, even the river-boats, which could have been used to convey much-needed rice and other foodstuffs to Calcutta and elsewhere in Bengal. Food prices skyrocketed, and throngs of hungry Bengalis flocked to the already overcrowded city of Calcutta. Calcutta's soup kitchens could not begin to keep up with the demands being placed on them, however, and between 1942 and 1944, hundreds of thousands of people died from starvation on the city's streets.

Although Mother Teresa was still supposed to be living a cloistered existence, Father Julien Henry, the head priest of St. Teresa's Church in Calcutta, recalled that she accompanied groups of her students on excursions into nearby slums during the war years. Presumably, she believed that "the emergency conditions made a strict interpretation of the rules of enclosure no longer tenable," wrote her biographer, Anne Sebba.[21] As Mother Teresa shepherded her charges through the squalor and filth, she would ask the girls: "Would you give a helping hand if someone began a service to help these poor people?"[22]

"I SAW THE BODIES ON THE STREETS"

The surrender of Japan and the end of World War II in August 1945 did not bring a halt to the enormous suffering and chaos that plagued Calcutta during the fighting. After the Indian people had clamored for self-rule for decades, they were finally about to achieve their independence from Great Britain. The prospect of freedom, however, had brought to the surface longstanding resentments between India's two major religious groups, the Hindus and the Muslims. Under the leadership of the Muslim League, the Muslims were determined to have their own homeland and demanded that the departing British divide the Indian subcontinent into two nations, Hindu India and Islamic Pakistan. In contrast, the predominantly Hindu Indian National Congress, under the direction of Mohandas Gandhi, wanted a united India.

Hoping to bring attention to their cause, the Muslim League declared August 16, 1946, a "Direct Action Day," in which Muslim Indians were to take to the streets to show their support for the partitioning of British India into two states. In Calcutta, where the population was split between Hindus and Muslims, the pro-partition demonstrations soon erupted into bloody riots, pitting one religious group against the other. By the time British forces finally restored order in the city, almost a week later,

Mohandas Gandhi, shown above in a photograph from 1947, led the Indian National Congress, which pressed for a united, independent India following World War II. Although Mother Teresa was never able to meet Gandhi, who was assassinated in 1948, she was impressed by his commitment to nonviolence.

at least 5,000 Calcuttans were dead, 15,000 wounded, and about 100,000 homeless.

While the violence raged on, all deliveries of food and other supplies within the city came to a standstill. At St. Mary's, Mother Teresa found herself with 300 hungry adolescents on her hands. "We were not supposed to go out into the streets, but I went anyway," she later revealed to Eileen Egan:

> Then I saw the bodies on the streets, stabbed, beaten, lying there in strange positions in their dried blood. We had been behind our safe walls. We knew that there had been rioting. People had been jumping over our walls, first a Hindu, then a Muslim. You see, our compound was between Moti Jihl, which was mainly Muslim then, and Tengra. . . . That was Hindu. We took in each one and helped him to escape safely. When I went out on the street—only then I saw the death that was following them. A lorry full of soldiers stopped me and told me I should not be out on the streets. No one should be out, they said. I told them I had to come out and take the risk. I had three hundred students who had nothing to eat. The soldiers had rice and they drove me back to the school and unloaded bags of rice.[23]

Just a few weeks after her disturbing first-hand encounter with Calcutta's bloodbath, Mother Teresa departed the battered city for the Himalayas and the Loreto convent at Darjeeling. Her health had been fragile as of late, and her superiors at Entally feared that she might have contracted tuberculosis. They ordered the 36-year-old nun to take a period of rest at the order's mountain retreat. As it turned out, Mother Teresa's train journey from Calcutta to Darjeeling on September 10, 1946, would prove to be one of the major turning points of her life.

CHAPTER 4

"A Call Within a Call"

On September 10, 1946, Mother Teresa was on the night train from Calcutta to the Loreto Sisters' Himalayan retreat at Darjeeling, when she suddenly heard a voice "speaking in her heart."[24] It was a heavenly summons, she believed: God was calling her to give up the comfortable world of the Loreto convent to live and labor in the slums of Calcutta. At first, Teresa had mixed feelings about what she would later describe as her "call within a call." She loved teaching at St. Mary's and regarded the nuns at Loreto Entally as her family. She knew she must do what the voice on the train had told her to do, though. "It was an order," she maintained. "To fail to obey would have been to break the faith."[25]

During her stay at the mountainside convent, Teresa said little to the other nuns and was obviously preoccupied. From time to time, she scrawled notes on a small pad of paper that she kept with her. When her period of rest at Darjeeling was over, Mother Teresa presented the notes to her spiritual adviser in Calcutta, Father Celeste Van Exem. In them, she outlined what she believed to be God's plan for her: She was to resign from the Loreto Order and establish a new missionary order dedicated to serving "the poorest of the poor. . . . The work was to be among the abandoned, those with nobody, the very poorest."[26]

OBTAINING PERMISSION FROM THE CHURCH

Convinced of the genuineness of Mother Teresa's "call within a call," Father Van Exem urged her to write to the head of the Calcutta Archdiocese, Archbishop Ferdinand Perier, asking for his assistance in obtaining the Church's approval for her plan. Perrier, however, had serious misgivings regarding Teresa's proposed mission. Not only was the archbishop worried about the effect that her abandonment of her order might have on the morale of the Loreto community, he also "did not relish the idea of a lone nun on Calcutta's streets," noted Eileen Eagan.[27] He informed Mother Teresa that he would have to ponder her proposal for at least one year before he decided whether he could support it.

At the end of 1947, although he was still skeptical about the wisdom of Mother Teresa's plan, Archbishop Perier allowed her to write to the head of the Loreto Sisters in Ireland to request her release from the order. The Mother General's reply two months later thrilled Mother Teresa. Persuaded that Teresa's call to live among India's destitute was "the will of God," the Mother General advised her to write to the Vatican at once.[28]

When Teresa presented the letter she had drafted to the Vatican to Archbishop Perier for review, however, he insisted that she make a critical modification to her proposal. Instead of asking the Vatican to grant her an indult (decree) of exclaustration, which would let her retain her sacred vows although she was no longer cloistered, he required that Teresa request an indult of secularization, which would make her a layperson. Mother Teresa was devastated by Perier's demand, as she had hoped to eventually found her own religious order. Nonetheless, she obediently revised her letter to the Holy See in accordance with the archbishop's wishes. Perier then sent the edited request to the

learned how to recognize the early signs of common illnesses, give injections, treat wounds, and deliver babies.

The Medical Mission Sisters also taught Mother Teresa how to properly care for herself after she started her labors in the slums. Originally, Teresa had planned to subsist on nothing more than rice and salt, just as Calcutta's poorest citizens did. The Sisters convinced the 38-year-old that her health and stamina were bound to suffer, however, if she failed to eat at least some protein every day. They also urged her to allow herself one full day of rest per week.

By December, Mother Teresa had completed her training in Patna and was anxious to return to Calcutta. First, however, she needed a place to sleep. With Archbishop Perier's assistance, Teresa soon found temporary shelter with the Little Sisters of the Poor, who ran a home for the elderly near Moti Jheel, the same slum where she hoped to inaugurate her mission.

Mother Teresa started her new enterprise in Moti Jheel just as India was launching its new life as an independent country, and the troubles of the infant nation's chief city—Calcutta—were multiplying. In August 1947, when Great Britain finally withdrew its forces from the Indian subcontinent, the former British territory had been divided into Hindu India and Muslim Pakistan, in accordance with the Muslim League's wishes. In the wake of the controversial partition, violence erupted between India and Pakistan, and millions of Hindus fled Muslim East Pakistan (now Bangladesh) for the already congested streets of Calcutta. Scores of new slums sprang up overnight, and all over the city people succumbed to cholera, typhoid, and starvation.

By the end of 1948, when Teresa embarked on her mission of mercy, historian Paul Williams noted, "Calcutta had the lowest life expectancy rate in the world."[30] Mother Teresa remained undaunted by the tremendous challenges facing her, however. She took courage from one of her favorite biblical passages: Chapter 4, Verse 13 of St. Paul's letter to the Philippians: "In Him who is the source of my strength I have strength for everything."[31]

SCHOOLS AND DISPENSARIES

When Mother Teresa began her work in Moti Jheel in December 1948, "she did not feel that it was necessary to carry out a survey or to make a plan or raise funds," wrote her biographer, Navin Chawla. "She simply saw that there was need for a school."[32] Because she had neither a building nor supplies, she taught her young pupils in a small open area among the rows of hovels, using a stick to trace the Bengali alphabet on the ground. Each day, her makeshift school attracted a few more students. Encouraged, Teresa started visiting Catholic churches and charitable societies to solicit donations for her undertaking. She must have been persuasive, because, in no time, Mother Teresa had collected enough money to rent space in a local building and purchase desks, blackboards, and books. Just a few weeks after she first walked into Moti Jheel, Teresa had more than 50 pupils and several volunteer teachers to assist her in instructing them.

Mother Teresa's work in Calcutta's slums was off to an impressive start, but she was not satisfied. With the Moti Jheel school up and running, she decided it was time to open a second free school in the even more notorious slum of Tiljala. By February 1949, Teresa had raised enough money to rent a room in a local building where she and a handful of volunteers taught some 25 boys and girls the rudiments of reading, writing, and arithmetic.

Mother Teresa quickly realized that the long-overlooked residents of Calcutta's poorest areas needed medical help as much as they needed schools. One of her first projects, therefore, was to open a medical dispensary in a room provided to her by St. Teresa's Church, near Moti Jheel. To keep her dispensary well stocked with medicine, she relied on donations from nearby pharmacies. When one local pharmacist declined to help, she stubbornly sat down on the floor of his shop and recited rosaries until he relented. (A rosary is a string of beads used by Catholics for counting a special sequence of prayers.) Soon, she had opened a medical dispensary in Tiljala as well, right next to her school.

THE MISSIONARIES OF CHARITY

In February 1949, Michael Gomes, a Roman Catholic Indian and admirer of Mother Teresa's charitable work, offered her the use of a large, second-floor room in his rambling house on Creek Lane, northwest of Loretto Entally. Now that she had a bit of space to call her own, Mother Teresa was eager to begin recruiting young women for the new order she hoped to found. Within a few weeks of moving to Creek Lane, Teresa had secured her first would-be novice, Subhashini Das, a well-off Bengali girl who had once been her student at St. Mary's.

Over the next few months, Teresa would recruit four more prospective nuns. Under Mother Teresa's direction, they taught

Day-to-Day Life Among the Sisters of Charity

Days in the mother house and on the teeming streets of Calcutta were "long and hard" for the members of the new Missionaries of Charity order, noted Mother Teresa's biographer:

During the week they rose at 4:40 A.M. to the call of *Benedicamus Domino* and the response of *Deo Gratias*. On Sundays the rising time was 4:15 A.M. They dressed at their bedsides with a sheet over their heads [for modesty's sake]. They went downstairs to wash their faces with water scooped out of tank in the courtyard with empty powdered milk tins, and collected ash from the stove in the kitchen with which to clean their teeth.

They washed themselves with a tablet of soap which had been divided into six and was used for washing both their clothes and their bodies. Morning prayers, meditation and Mass consumed the time between 5:15 and 6:45 A.M. . . . They were made to eat quickly and to take a vitamin pill, and by 7:45 A.M. they were out into the streets of Calcutta to work amongst the poorest of the poor, having somehow managed, with the limited facilities available, to have their obligatory daily bath and wash all the previous day's clothes in a bucket. Shortly after noon they returned to the mother house for prayers, a meal

the young, cared for the sick, fed the hungry, and prayed with the dying and bereaved of Moti Jheel and Tiljala. All the young women resided at the Gomes's house, where their new Mother Superior closely regulated their lives with a bell system for working, praying, eating, and sleeping. Like Teresa, they dressed in simple white saris with blue borders, instead of more traditional, European-style religious habits.

By late 1949, Mother Teresa's year of probation had come to an end. Nearly a dozen followers now lived with her in the house on Creek Lane and assisted her in her work with Calcutta's poorest citizens. Impressed by all that Teresa had been able to accomplish in just 12 months, Archbishop Perier told her she had passed her

of five ladles of bulgar wheat and three bits of meat if meat was available. After lunch there was housework to be done, and then Mother Teresa was very insistent that they should have a rest for half an hour. Afterwards they had prayers and afternoon tea, which consisted of two dry chapattis [an Indian flatbread] followed by half an hour of spiritual reading and instruction from Mother Teresa. Then it was back to their duties in the city. At six they returned to the mother house for prayers and adoration of the sacrament, followed by a meal of rice, dhal [a lentil dish], and vegetables, during which they had ten minutes of spiritual reading. Then came time for mending—using a razor blade, needle and darning thread contained in a cigarette tin—and recreation before evening prayers and bed by ten o'clock. Recreation was one of the few times at which conversation was permitted other than for communication essential to the work. The signal for them to be free to talk was the invitation *Laudetur Jesus Christus* to which the response "Amen" was sometimes almost shouted with relief at the opportunity to share some of the experiences of the day.*

*Kathryn Spink, *Mother Teresa: A Complete Authorized Biography*. San Francisco: HarperCollins, 1997, p. 46.

probationary period with flying colors. He also assured her that he would do everything in his power to gain official recognition for her little flock as a Catholic religious order. If Teresa would supply him with a constitution for the proposed congregation, he said, he would personally present the document to the appropriate Vatican officials when he visited Rome the following April.

The constitution Mother Teresa ultimately devised was unique; it added a fourth vow to the traditional three professed by all Catholic nuns. Members of the Missionaries of Charity, as she named her proposed order, would not only be obliged to take vows of poverty, chastity, and obedience, but also must pledge "to give wholehearted and free service to the poorest of the poor."[33]

On October 7, 1950, six months after Perier presented their constitution to the Vatican, the little band at Creek Lane received papal approval as a new congregation. Over the next two years, the order attracted nearly 30 members. Clearly, the Missionaries of Charity needed bigger quarters. In early 1953, Mother Teresa and her group departed the crowded Gomes residence for an airy three-story house on Lower Circular Road (today called Acharya Jagdish Chandra Bose Road), in the heart of Calcutta. The Catholic archdiocese of Calcutta had provided the funds to purchase the home, which it obtained for a modest price from a Muslim physician who planned to move to Pakistan.

The Missionaries of Charity had always been committed to a life of rigorous poverty, and this did not change after they moved into their spacious new facility. Each resident of the new mother house—Mother Teresa included—kept her worldly belongings to a bare minimum: three cotton saris, a pair of sandals, a crucifix and rosary, an umbrella for the monsoon season, a bucket for washing, and a thin straw-filled pad to sleep on.

NIRMAL HRIDAY

Around the time of their move to the new mother house, the Missionaries of Charity launched a major new undertaking: a home

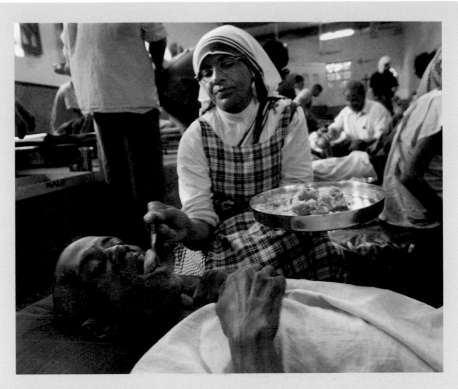

A nun, a member of the Missionaries of Charity, feeds an ill Indian man at the Nirmal Hriday Home for the destitute and dying. This photograph, taken in 2003, shows how Mother Teresa's mission has persisted since her death in 1997.

for the dying indigent. Mother Teresa first resolved to open such a facility after failing to convince several local hospitals to admit a dying woman whom she had discovered lying in a gutter, her feet half eaten away by rats. Since their facilities had only a limited number of free beds for indigents, the hospital administrators informed Mother Teresa that granting that precious space to anybody who was obviously beyond recovery made no sense. The very next day, Teresa launched a crusade to convince Calcutta's health department to give her a place where she could help the city's destitute "die with dignity and love."[34] "They have lived like beasts," she told the officials. "At least they ought to die like human beings.[35]

In response to Mother Teresa's persistent campaign, the health department offered the Missionaries of Charity the use of a vacant building in the bustling Kalighat section of Calcutta. Mother Teresa christened her new house for the dying *Nirmal Hriday,* which is Bengali for "Place of the Pure Heart." The building was once a shelter for Hindu pilgrims visiting the nearby temple of the goddess of Kali and stood right next to a funeral pyre. Because of its proximity to the Kali Temple, the pyre adjoining Nirmal Hriday was considered to be one of the holiest spots in Calcutta for a Hindu to be cremated.

When Nirmal Hriday first opened its doors on August 22, 1952, the Hindu priests at the Kali Temple viewed the facility and its staff with apprehension. Rumors had been circulating that the Sisters' real motive for taking in the dying poor of Calcutta was not to offer them a measure of dignity or comfort in their last hours but to convert them to Catholicism. In truth, the priests need not have worried, because Mother Teresa consistently refused to force her personal religious beliefs on anyone. "There is only one God," she liked to say, "and He is the God of everyone. So it's important that all men and women be looked upon as equal in the sight of God. I have always said that we should help a Hindu become a better Hindu, a Muslim become a better Muslim, and a Catholic become a better Catholic."[36]

Despite Teresa's commitment to religious tolerance, however, her priestly neighbors at Kalighat remained suspicious of the Missionaries of Charity. They complained that it was inappropriate for the nuns to be working in proximity to one of their faith's holiest shrines, and they repeatedly petitioned city officials to evict the Sisters. When Mother Teresa and her staff at Nirmal Hriday lovingly cared for a mortally ill Kali priest who had been one of their harshest critics, however, the dying man's colleagues had a change of heart regarding the nuns and their diminutive Mother Superior. Like many of their fellow Calcuttans—Hindu, Muslim, and Christian alike—the priests at Kali were beginning to see Mother Teresa as one of their city's chief treasures, a woman of remarkable compassion and devotion.

MINISTERING TO CALCUTTA'S ABANDONED AND REJECTED

Within a year of opening Nirmal Hriday, Mother Teresa had embarked on another major charitable project in Calcutta, the Shishu Bhavan home for abandoned and orphaned children. Located in a renovated house just one block from the mother house, by 1958 Shishu Bhavan was home to nearly 100 boys and girls.

The Missionaries of Charity next turned their attention to Calcutta's substantial leper population. Leprosy is a chronic infectious disease that primarily affects the skin and nerves. It is most common in tropical and subtropical climates. If the disease is left untreated, sufferers often experience disfiguring skin sores and nerve damage, which can lead to a complete loss of sensation in their hands and feet. Because they cannot feel pain, lepers tend to inadvertently injure themselves; this often results in crippling deformities. Throughout much of human history, leprosy was among the most feared of all communicable diseases, and its victims were compelled to live apart from the community. Leprosy also carried with it a high degree of social stigma, because many religions—including Hinduism—taught that the illness was a form of divine punishment for especially sinful behavior.

Mother Teresa first decided to work with Calcutta's downtrodden leper community in 1957, when a group of infected men arrived at the door of the mother house in desperate need of food and shelter. Mother Teresa learned that, when it became evident that the men had the disease, they were fired from their jobs and banned from their neighborhoods. Even their own families treated them as outcasts. Like the vast majority of Calcutta's 30,000 lepers, the men never received medical treatment, although drugs

Street urchins sell flowers on the main street of Calcutta, near St. Thomas' Church, where Mother Teresa's body was laid in state after her death. Mother Teresa labored for years to help children such as these.

capable of slowing or even halting the disease's progress had been available for more than a decade.

Mother Teresa was determined to get medicine and other much needed assistance to the tens of thousands of men, women, and children in her city affected by the disease, so she launched an energetic fundraising campaign to create a mobile leper clinic. With the money collected, the Missionaries of Charity converted a donated ambulance into a traveling medical dispensary. Staffed by members of the order as well as by volunteers, the mobile clinic went on weekly missions into Calcutta's slums, bringing drugs, disinfectants, bandages, food, and other essential supplies to leprosy victims of all ages.

Convinced that the lepers' greatest problem was emotional—the feeling of being unloved and unwanted—Mother Teresa and her workers always made it a point to treat their disfigured patients with compassion and warmth. Eventually, the Missionaries of Charity founded a leper colony outside the city of Calcutta, where those afflicted with the disease could lead productive and largely self-sufficient lives while receiving regular medical treatment. At the colony, lepers resided in their own homes and either farmed or learned a skilled trade, such as weaving.

NEW PARTNERSHIPS

Throughout the 1950s, while Mother Teresa expanded her ministry to include the dying destitute, orphaned and abandoned children, and lepers, she was also building important new partnerships with lay volunteers in India and Europe. Two of the most fruitful of these relationships were with Jacqueline De Decker and Ann Blaikie.

Teresa first met De Decker in late 1948, when she was interning with the Medical Mission Sisters in Patna, in preparation to begin her work in Calcutta's slums. De Decker, who also felt drawn to India's destitute, was intrigued by Mother Teresa's plan to create a new charitable order to serve the poorest of the poor. To her sorrow, however, an increasingly debilitating and painful spinal condition prevented Jacqueline De Decker from joining the Missionaries of Charity. Forced to return home to Belgium for medical treatment, De Decker underwent multiple surgeries, none of which was able to relieve her intense back pain.

Mother Teresa realized how eager De Decker was to further her cause, so, in 1952, she invited her Belgian friend to form a new branch of the Missionaries of Charity, the Sick and Suffering Co-Workers. The new organization linked an ill or disabled individual who wished to support Mother Teresa's work with a Sister from the Missionaries of Charity to be prayer partners. Convinced that there was enormous spiritual power in human suffering, Mother

Influences on the Peacemaker

Jesus Christ

Above all else, Mother Teresa's devotion to peace was firmly grounded in her Christian faith. "Blessed are the peacemakers, for they shall be called sons of God," declared Jesus. (Matthew 5:9) "You have heard that it was said, 'You shall love your neighbor and hate your enemy.' But I say to you, 'Love your enemies and pray for those who persecute you, so that you may be sons of your Father who is in heaven,'" he admonished his followers. (Matthew 5:43–45)

Mother Teresa was committed to living her life according to Jesus's commandment: "As I have loved you so you must love one another." (John 13:34) Mother Teresa was also convinced, though, that only when all people learned to love their neighbors just as God loved them could lasting peace on earth be achieved. The Heavenly Father wanted all His children to be united in a single human community without borders, she asserted. "If we have no peace," she said, "it is because we have forgotten that we belong to each other—that man, that woman, that child, is my brother or my sister."* Therefore, Mother Teresa contended, it followed that works of charity and love toward fellow humans were also works of peace.

Mohandas Gandhi

Mother Teresa's lifelong devotion to nonviolence and serving the poor may also have been shaped by the great Indian hero Mohandas K. Gandhi. Born into a devout Hindu family in western India in 1869, Gandhi became one of the most revered political and spiritual leaders of modern times. He used community meetings and boycotts, marches, letters, fasting, and prayer to developed a system of nonviolent resistance that was to play a central role in ending British rule in India after World War II.

Mother Teresa never had the opportunity to meet Gandhi, who was assassinated in January 1948. She was well aware of Gandhi's philosophy and career and deeply respected him for his nonviolent principles and compassion for society's forgotten, including lepers.

A decade after Gandhi's death, she named her groundbreaking center for lepers in Titlagarh, India, *Gandhi Prem Niwas* ("Gandhi Center for Love"), in his honor.

Gandhi's use of symbolism as a means of calling attention to the plight of India's poor and dispossessed clearly influenced Mother Teresa, according to Indian author Navin Chawla. Gandhi became famous for shunning all earthly possessions and dressing in a handspun loincloth and shawl, like the most destitute of Indian males. When Mother Teresa left the Loreto compound, Chawla noted, she followed Gandhi's example by donning a simple white sari similar to those worn by the poor women with whom she lived. Through adopting the attire of India's most impoverished citizens, Gandhi and Mother Teresa demonstrated their solidarity with the people whom Gandhi named the *daridra narayans* ("the homeless, the voiceless, and the unwanted"). "How can I look the poor in the eye," Mother Teresa once asked, "How could I tell them, 'I love you and understand you,' if I didn't live as they do?"**

Throughout her life Mother Teresa consistently relied on non-violent resistance in the face of conflict. When she first opened Nirmal Hriday in the Kalighat section of Calcutta, some local Hindus were bitterly opposed to her new home for the dying because of its proximity to one of India's most revered Hindu shrines, the Kali Temple. According to one account, one day several young men burst into the center and angrily demanded that the center be closed immediately. Instead of trying to argue with the intruders, Mother Teresa quietly continued to minister to her patients. When the protestors saw the compassion and respect with which she and her Sisters treated the filthy, sore-ridden men and women whom they had rescued from Calcutta's streets and gutters, the men departed without a word and did not return.

---

*David Scott, *A Revolution of Love: The Meaning of Mother Teresa*. Chicago: Loyola Press, p. 139.

**Christian Feldman, *Mother Teresa: Love Stays*. New York: Crossroad Publishing, 1998, p. 128.

with the poor, sick, and forgotten of India began to appear regularly in Catholic publications. As the first year of the new decade drew to a close, Mother Teresa and her Missionaries of Charity were about to enter a period of unprecedented international influence and fame.

CHAPTER 5

Becoming
an International
Figure

I n February 1965, after four years of determined campaigning by Mother Teresa, Pope Paul VI declared the Missionaries of Charity to be a "society of pontifical right." This meant that her congregation would answer directly to the Vatican rather than to the Archbishop of Calcutta. For the first time ever, the Missionaries of Charity would be able carry their work beyond India's borders; only the Vatican could grant members of a Catholic religious order permission to live and labor in other countries.

COCOROTE, VENEZUELA: FIRST OVERSEAS MISSION

Within six months of coming under Vatican jurisdiction, the Missionaries of Charity established their first house outside of India in the Venezuelan diocese of Barquisimeto, at the invitation of a local churchman, Bishop Benitez. Impressed by Mother Teresa's charitable endeavors in India, Benitez wanted her to assist the "poorest of the poor" in his own backyard: the landless and largely illiterate descendants of African slaves who had been imported by the Spanish

Mother Teresa kneels before Pope Paul VI during a 1971 visit to the Vatican. This trip took place six years after Pope Paul declared the Missionaries of Charity to be a "society of pontifical right," answering directly to the Vatican.

centuries earlier to toil in the copper mines of Barquisimeto's "Zona Negra" (Black Belt) section.

After visiting and evaluating the Zona Negra region herself, Mother Teresa decided to send a team of nuns to the little town of Cocorote, where an unoccupied Catholic rectory could serve as their convent. The Sisters quickly resolved to devote most of their time and efforts to the Zona Negra's downtrodden female population. Within the Afro-Venezuelan community of the Zona Negra, it was common for a man to take several wives. Even though their husbands often had more wives and offspring than they could possibly support, the women of the Zona Negra were expected to focus all of their energies on housekeeping and childcare.

Dismayed by the degrading poverty under which many women and children in the region were compelled to live, the Missionaries of Charity decided to provide basic vocational training to the Zona Negra's female inhabitants. To help make the women more economically self-sufficient, the Sisters instructed them in such practical skills as sewing and typing. They utilized an abandoned Cocorote hotel that had been donated to the order. The cloth, sewing machines, and typewriters the Sisters used were supplied by the Diocesan Council of Catholic Women of Brooklyn, New York, which agreed to sponsor the faraway mission after hearing Mother Teresa lecture on her order's Venezuelan mission.

A GROWING INTERNATIONAL PRESENCE

During the 1960s, Mother Teresa's first overseas venture was soon followed by invitations to found missions in a number of locations around the globe, from Ceylon (now Sri Lanka), off the coast of India, to the African nation of Tanzania, to the Middle Eastern kingdom of Jordan, to Australia. In these far-flung places, the Missionaries of Charities tirelessly devoted themselves to aiding the destitute, the diseased, the abandoned, and the dying, just as they had done in India.

In 1968, Mother Teresa received an overseas invitation that greatly surprised her: Pope Paul VI asked the Missionaries of Charity to set up a branch in Rome. Rome was home to dozens of Catholic religious orders, so Mother Teresa found it hard to believe that her Sisters were really needed in the "Eternal City." After touring Rome's squalid suburbs and observing firsthand the abject poverty of the inhabitants, however, Mother Teresa realized that there was more than enough work for her nuns to do there. In keeping with her belief that her Sisters should live among the people they served, she purchased a humble shack in one of Rome's worst slums to serve as a convent. From their ramshackle headquarters, the Missionaries of Charity tutored the young, visited the sick, and fed the hungry, focusing particularly on the city's poorest of the poor: the refugees from Italy's depressed southern provinces of Sardinia and Sicily, who flocked to Rome during the 1960s and 1970s in a desperate—and generally fruitless—search for employment.

Two years after founding her Roman mission, Mother Teresa traveled to London to open a training center for new recruits to the Missionaries of Charity—the order's first novitiate outside of India. While in London, she spent many hours among the drug addicts, alcoholics, mentally ill, and other "down-and-outs" who made up the city's large homeless population. The fact that there was so much misery and degradation in one of the world's wealthiest countries dismayed her. "Here you have the Welfare State," she noted to a British acquaintance. "Nobody need starve. But there is a different poverty: The poverty of the spirit, of loneliness and being unwanted."[38] In an effort to address this "poverty of the spirit," Mother Teresa opened several "Homes of Compassion" in London. The homes' staff brought food, blankets, and medicine to the homeless; knocked on the doors of the elderly and shut-ins; and generally attempted "to touch areas of human suffering from which others shied away," as Mother Teresa put it.[39]

Mother Teresa's belief that even the richest nations in the world needed her assistance led her, in 1971, to open a convent in the heart of one of New York City's most crime-ridden neighborhoods, the South Bronx. Isolation and constant fear was a way of life for many of the borough's residents, particularly the elderly. On one occasion, when her Sisters were visiting a run-down tenement that was home to a number of elderly shut-ins, Mother Teresa told Eileen Egan:

> They came to a room from which a bad odor was coming. When the room was broken into, they found a woman who had been dead four or five days. No one had come to see her. They did not even know her name. Many of the people are known only by the numbers of their rooms or apartments. One of the greatest of diseases is to be nobody to no one.[40]

A HUMANITARIAN CRISIS AND A PERSONAL TRAGEDY

Around the same time that the Missionaries of Charity opened their new mission in the South Bronx, a major humanitarian crisis was developing in East Pakistan, soon to be renamed Bangladesh. Ever since the partition of India, resentments had been growing between West and East Pakistan. The residents of these two areas were divided not only by geography but also by language and ethnic origin. The rift between the two Pakistani provinces grew in 1970, when East Pakistan was hit by a massive cyclone that killed 300,000 people and caused extensive property damage.

Angered by what they viewed as West Pakistan's callous indifference to their plight, in early 1971, the leaders of East Pakistan, with the backing of the Indian government, declared their region's independence. Soon afterward, West Pakistani troops invaded the already devastated province. Although the war, which resulted in the creation of the independent nation of Bangladesh, lasted just nine months, it had grave consequences for India, particularly for Mother Teresa's hometown of Calcutta. During the fighting, millions of refugees fled East Pakistan for India, with about 250,000 of them ending up in Calcutta, a city that had already been forced to absorb thousands of refugees following the great cyclone of 1970.

Working in conjunction with the Indian government, the United Nations, Catholic Relief Services, and a host of other international organizations, Mother Teresa and her Missionaries of Charity did their best to address the needs of the impoverished and often diseased refugees, particularly the tens of thousands of displaced children. Immediately after the war's end, Mother Teresa also took a team of her Sisters into the new nation of Bangladesh, where they established centers in those areas that were hardest hit by the violence.

In the wake of the Bangladesh crisis, Mother Teresa experienced a bitter personal disappointment. For years, she had been trying to gain permission from Albania's totalitarian government to visit her mother and sister, who had moved from Skopje to Tirana during the early 1930s to be near Lazar Bojaxhiu. When Benito Mussolini's troops occupied Albania in 1939, though, Bojaxhiu had joined the fascist dictator's army and ended up spending World War II in Italy. At the end of the war, Albania fell under Communist rule, and anyone who had cooperated with the Italian occupiers was branded a traitor. Barred from ever

Mother Teresa in Her Own Words

On Generosity

I ask you one thing: do not tire of giving, but do not give your leftovers. Give until it hurts, until you feel the pain.

We should learn how to give. But we should not regard giving as an obligation, but as a desire. I usually say to our Co-Workers: "I do not need your surplus. I do not want you to give me your leftovers. Our poor do not need your condescending attitude nor your pity. The poor need your love and your kindness."

On Christ in the Poor

Whoever the poorest of the poor are, they are Christ for us— Christ under the guise of human suffering.

When a poor person dies of hunger, it has not happened because God did not take care of him or her. It has happened because neither you nor I wanted to give that person what he or she needed. We have refused to be instruments of love in the hands of God to give the poor a piece of bread, to offer them a dress with which to ward off the cold. It has happened because we did not recognize Christ when, once more, he appeared under the guise of pain, identified with a man numb from the cold, dying of hunger, when he came in a lonely human being, in a lost child in search of a home.

On Love

All sicknesses have cures. The only one that cannot be cured is the sickness of feeling unloved. I invite all those who appreciate

returning home, Bojaxhiu decided to settle permanently in Italy, where he soon married and started a family.

During the 1960s, Mother Teresa had met with her older brother and his family in Italy on several occasions, but she had not seen his mother or his sister since 1929, when she left Skopje to join the Loreto Sisters. When she heard that her mother had fallen gravely ill and that her dying wish was to see "Agnes" and

our work to look around them and be willing to love those who have no love and to offer them their services. Are we not, by definition, messengers of love?

God has created us so we do small things with great love. I believe that great love, that comes, or should come from our heart, should start at home: with my family, my neighbors across the street, those right next door. And this love should then reach everyone.

On Life and Death
In my heart, I carry the last glances of the dying. I do all I can so that they feel loved at that most important moment when a seemingly useless existence can be redeemed.

On Loneliness
There are many kinds of poverty. Even in countries where the economic situation seems to be a good one, there are expressions of poverty hidden in a deep place, such as the tremendous loneliness of people who have been abandoned and who are suffering.

As far as I am concerned, the greatest suffering is to feel alone, unwanted, unloved. The greatest suffering is also having no one, forgetting what an intimate, truly human relationship is, not knowing what it means to be loved, not having a family or friends.*

---

*Mother Teresa, and José Louis Ganzález-Balado, compiler, *Mother Teresa: In My Own Words*. Liguori, Mo.: Liguori Publications, 1989, pp. 17, 19, 24, 25, 38, 45, 70, 91.

Lazar one more time, Teresa redoubled her efforts to visit her mother, but to no avail. In July 1972, Mother Teresa received the heartbreaking news that her mother had died. Almost exactly one year later, in August 1973, her grief was compounded when she learned that her sister had died in Tirana, as well.

THE MISSIONARY BROTHERS OF CHARITY

While Mother Teresa was expanding her congregation's work to include countries outside of India, she was also expanding her mission in a different direction. During the early 1960s, she became increasingly convinced that men had a vital role to play in her crusade to help the poorest of the poor. The hundreds of frightened and homeless boys who came to Calcutta each year in search of food and work particularly needed adult male supervision, she believed. To Mother Teresa's relief, the archbishop of Calcutta found her arguments for creating a male branch of her religious order persuasive; in 1963, he authorized her to found the Missionary Brothers of Charity.

Although the group started out with just a handful of members, after the appointment of the charismatic Australian priest Ian Travers-Ball as director of the order in 1966, the Missionary Brothers grew rapidly. (Mother Teresa could not serve as director, as the Catholic Church forbids women from supervising male congregations.) Under the leadership of Travers-Ball—or Brother Andrew as he was then known—the new missionary order focused its attention on Calcutta's destitute male population, especially the chronically ill and dying, abandoned and orphaned children, and lepers.

Following in Mother Teresa's footsteps, by the early 1970s, the Brothers of Charity had taken their mission to the poor beyond India's borders. Their first foreign venture was in the war-ravaged country of Vietnam, where they established a house in Saigon in early 1973 to feed and shelter the city's destitute. By 1975, however, the house had been shut down, and the

Mother Teresa, left, accepts a profession of vows from a nun at St. Peter's Cathedral in San Francisco, California. By the early 1970s, Mother Teresa oversaw 80 missions in locations all over the globe.

Brothers were deported by Vietnam's new Communist regime. Undaunted, the Brothers focused on new overseas projects, setting up houses in Taiwan, Korea, the Philippines, Brazil, Haiti, Guatemala, the United States, and other countries.

MOTHER TERESA'S GROWING FAME

By the early 1970s, Mother Teresa, who now oversaw some 80 houses in locations all over the globe, was well on her way to becoming a major international celebrity. In stark contrast to other Catholic religious orders after World War II, the Missionaries of Charity was growing by leaps and bounds, accepting 139 new members in 1970 alone. Postulants came from every region of India, as well as a host of other countries, including Ireland, Great Britain, the United States, Italy, Yugoslavia, Pakistan, and Venezuela. Mother Teresa had been an Indian citizen since 1948; by the 1970s, her stature in her adopted country was such that Prime Minister Indira Gandhi awarded her a free pass on Air India to offset the cost of her frequent journeys abroad to lecture, open new missions, or check on existing centers.

At least some of the credit for Mother Teresa's budding international reputation during the 1970s goes to British journalist and Roman Catholic convert Malcolm Muggeridge. In 1968, Muggeridge was asked by the British Broadcasting Corporation (BBC) to conduct a brief televised interview with Mother Teresa in London. The English viewing audience was deeply moved by the diminutive nun's account of her work with the destitute and dying in India, and letters of support and monetary donations for the Missionaries of Charity poured into the BBC.

Perhaps the most devoted of Mother Teresa's growing legion of British fans, however, was Muggeridge himself. In 1969, he persuaded Teresa to let him make an hour-long documentary film about her work in Calcutta. Entitled *Something Beautiful for God,* the film attracted a wide and enthusiastic audience. In 1971, Muggeridge published a book by the same title. In it, he recounted his experiences while making the documentary; the book, too, was a huge success. In his conclusion, Muggeridge had this to say about Mother Teresa:

> It will be for posterity to decide whether she is a saint. I only say of her that in a dark time she is a burning and a shining light; in a cruel time, a living embodiment of Christ's gospel of love; in a godless time, the Word dwelling among us, full of grace and truth. For this, all who have the inestimable privilege of knowing her, or knowing of her, must be eternally grateful.[41]

In the wake of the positive publicity for her work generated by Muggeridge's film and book, Mother Teresa found herself the

Mother Teresa is shown here during a visit to Belfast, Ireland, in 1971. The Sisters of Loreto, the first order to which Mother Teresa belonged, is based in Ireland.

recipient of a series of prestigious international awards. In 1971, Pope Paul VI presented her with the Pope John XXIII Peace Prize, which honored those who worked to promote peace, love, justice, and truth among individuals or nations. Three other major awards followed that same year: the Good Samaritan Award of the National Catholic Development Conference, the John F. Kennedy International Award, and an honorary degree from the Catholic University of America. In 1972, the Indian government honored her with the Nehru Award for International Understanding, and in 1973 Prince Philip of England awarded her the Templeton Award for Progress in Religion. The recognition and cash rewards these various awards entailed allowed Mother Teresa to open additional houses, including the Nirmala Kennedy Center in Calcutta for mentally or physically handicapped children.

THE CAMPAIGN FOR THE NOBEL PEACE PRIZE

Many in Mother Teresa's growing legion of admirers during the 1970s, especially Malcolm Muggeridge, were convinced that she was worthy of an even more prestigious award than any she had been granted thus far: the Nobel Peace Prize. In 1972, Muggeridge persuaded Lester Pearson, a Peace Prize laureate and the former prime minister of Canada, to submit Mother Teresa's name to the Nobel Committee. Neither she nor any of the other nominees in 1972 was granted the prize, however. (The Nobel Peace Prize is not awarded every year.)

Muggeridge was not about to give up easily on his crusade to secure the ultimate accolade for the woman he viewed as the embodiment of Christ's gospel of love. In 1975, Shirley Williams, a member of the British Parliament, nominated Mother Teresa for the Peace Prize at Muggeridge's urging. Several prominent North American statesmen seconded the nomination, including U.S. Senators Edward Kennedy, Hubert Humphrey, Mark Hatfield, and Pete Domenici; Canadian Maurice Strong, the head of the UN Environmental Program; and Robert McNamara, president of the World Bank and a former U.S. secretary of defense. (The World Bank is dedicated to reducing global poverty and improving living standards. The organization grants low-interest loans and interest-free credit to developing nations for health, infrastructure, education, and other purposes.)

A number of influential religious organizations also endorsed Mother Teresa; these included the National Council of Catholic Women and the National Council of the Churches of Christ, an interdenominational group comprising representatives from Protestant, evangelical, and Orthodox churches in the United States. Despite these impressive efforts on her behalf, however, the Nobel Committee overlooked Mother Teresa once again, awarding the 1975 Peace Prize to Russian human rights advocate Andrei Sakharov.

Two years later, Mother Teresa's name was resubmitted to the Nobel committee, this time by respected British author and environmentalist Barbara Ward. When the award went instead to the human rights organization Amnesty International, Mother Teresa joked good-naturedly to reporters about the prize and the check for $190,000 that went with it: "I had a good laugh over the Nobel Prize. It will come only when Jesus thinks it is time. We have all calculated to build two hundred homes for the lepers if it comes, so our people will have to do a lot of praying."[42]

On October 16, 1979, seven years after first being nominated for the Nobel Peace Prize, Mother Teresa was finally declared the recipient of the award. Although the name of her nominator that year has yet to be divulged, it is generally assumed to have been Robert McNamara, of the World Bank. In 1975, McNamara had written eloquently of Mother Teresa:

> Many public personalities—government officials, diplomats, members of international communities, and others—advance the cause of peace, and deserve recognition. But I believe that Mother Teresa merits the unique honor of the Nobel Peace Prize because she advances peace in the most fundamental way possible: by her extraordinary reaffirmation of the inviolability of human dignity. She does so by serving the needs of the absolute poor—the poor who are so disadvantaged that they have nowhere else to turn. She serves them irrespective of their religion, their race, their nationality, or their political beliefs. She serves them simply because of their intrinsic worth as individual human beings. Her work is not sentimental. It is realistic and effective. And it is expanding. A growing number of others around the world—in an international ecumenical association, the Coworkers of Mother Teresa—are undertaking similar efforts under her inspiration. But more important than the organizational structure of her work is the message it conveys that genuine peace is not the mere absence of hostilities, but rather the tranquility that arises out of a social order in which individuals treat one another with justice and compassion.[43]

The chairman of the Norwegian Nobel Peace Prize Committee, John Sanness (right), hands the Peace Prize diploma and gold medal to Mother Teresa. Mother Teresa was awarded the 1979 Nobel Peace Prize, which she accepted "in the name of the poor, the hungry, the sick and the lonely."

Immediately after the announcement of the Nobel Peace Prize recipient in Oslo, dozens of journalists descended on the mother house in Calcutta to record Mother Teresa's response to this great honor. "I am unworthy," she told them, "but thank God for this blessed gift for the poor."[44]

"IN THE NAME OF THE POOR"

On December 8, 1979, Mother Teresa arrived in Oslo, Norway, accompanied by her very first two postulants in Calcutta, Sister Agnes and Sister Gertrude. Two days later at Oslo University, Mother Teresa accepted the Nobel Peace Prize and the $190,000 check "unworthily but gratefully in the name of the poor, the hungry, the sick and the lonely."[45] An additional $6,000 would also be donated to the poor of Calcutta by the Nobel Committee: the sum that would have been spent on a ceremonial banquet if Mother Teresa had not cancelled the dinner, declaring that she preferred the money be used to buy food for those who actually needed it.

John Sannes, the chair of the Nobel committee, introduced Mother Teresa to the 800 guests who had gathered at the university that day. In explaining why the committee had chosen Mother Teresa from among the other distinguished nominees for the award, he said:

> The year 1979 has not been a year of peace. Disputes and conflicts between nations, peoples and ideologies have been conducted with all the accompanying extremes of inhumanity and cruelty. We have witnessed wars, the unrestrained use of violence; we have witnessed fanaticism hand in hand with cynicism; we have witnessed contempt for human life and dignity. . . . The Norwegian Nobel Committee has considered it right and appropriate, precisely in this year, in their choice of Mother Teresa to remind the world of the words spoken by Fridtjof Nansen: "Love of one's neighbor is realistic policy."

As a description of Mother Teresa's life's work we might select the slogan that a previous Nobel Peace Prize Laureate, Albert Schweitzer, adopted as the leitmotif for his own work: "Veneration for Life." . . .

In awarding Nobel's Prize for 1979 to Mother Teresa, the Committee has posed a focal question . . . Can any political, social, or intellectual feat of engineering, on the international or on the national plane, however effective and rational, however idealistic and principled its protagonists may be, give us anything but a house built on a foundation of sand, unless the spirit of Mother Teresa inspires the builders and takes its dwelling in their building?[46]

After leading the audience in prayer, Mother Teresa told her listeners that the Good News proclaimed by Jesus Christ "was peace to all men of good will, and this is something that we all want—the peace of heart." Then she plunged directly into the central theme of her speech, the evils of abortion: "We are talking about peace, but, I feel that the greatest destroyer of peace today is abortion. Because it is a direct war, a direct killing—direct murder by the mother herself." She also came out strongly in favor of "natural family planning" and against artificial contraception, which, like abortion, is officially opposed by the Roman Catholic Church.[47]

"The speech was controversial," wrote Anne Sebba.

But Mother Teresa was giving notice that here was an issue she was never going to go soft on, one on which she would never lose an opportunity to proclaim her views. In spite of her acceptance of natural family planning, she would never understand those who felt with a moral conviction equal to hers that the world might be a better place if it were less populated.[48]

If some in the audience that day were offended by Mother Teresa's tirade against abortion and artificial contraception, the

Critics of the Peacemaker

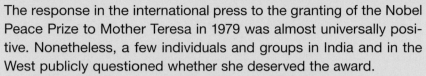

The response in the international press to the granting of the Nobel Peace Prize to Mother Teresa in 1979 was almost universally positive. Nonetheless, a few individuals and groups in India and in the West publicly questioned whether she deserved the award.

For the most part, the Indian press was thrilled with the selection of Mother Teresa, a naturalized Indian citizen, for the prestigious Nobel Peace Prize. One editorial in a left-wing publication entitled "Nothing Noble About Nobel," however, argued that Mother Teresa did not merit the award because she was little more than a spiritual colonizer, more concerned about converting India's poor to her Western faith than in genuinely improving the quality of their lives. "For when all is said and done," the editorialist accused, "she is a missionary. In serving the poor and the sick, her sole objective is to influence people in favor of Christianity and, if possible, to convert them. Missionaries are instruments of Western imperialist countries—and not innocent voices of God." Her charitable endeavors, the article went on, were therefore unworthy of the Indian term *nishkama seva*, meaning "selfless service without hope of reward."*

Mother Teresa's longstanding campaign against abortion and artificial contraception caused others, particularly in the West, to question whether she should have been awarded the Nobel Peace Prize. Because of her blind devotion to the Catholic Church's official position on birth control, her opponents argued, Mother Teresa refused to admit the grave problems that overpopulation had created in India and other Third World countries. One of the last things that impoverished and densely populated nations like India needed was a crusade against family planning, they asserted.

In her Nobel Peace Prize lecture, Mother Teresa denounced artificial contraception and identified abortion as the single greatest threat to peace in the contemporary world. In sharp contrast, her critics insisted that overpopulation and the poverty, competition for scarce resources, and the political instability that it can spawn seriously undermine world peace. Therefore, they said, responsible

(continues)

(continued)

private charities and governments alike in Third World nations ought to promote rather than discourage family planning practices and strive to make birth control services available to all citizens.

A final factor in people's belief that Mother Teresa should not have received the world's leading peace award was that she never concerned herself with the social or economic roots of poverty. She only thought in terms of fighting poverty through individual moral reform by encouraging people to be more generous and loving, and less materialistic. Identifying the fundamental social and economic causes of poverty and using that knowledge to reform inequitable social, economic, and political structures did not interest her. Moreover, her critics asserted, Mother Teresa's emphasis on helping the individual rather than promoting broad programs of social justice or economic development meant that her charitable activities would never amount to anything more than tiny drops in a veritable ocean of need and misery.

This line of criticism did not faze Mother Teresa in the least, however. She simply did not have "the time to think about grand programs," she once remarked. What her work was all about "is the person. To be able to love the individual, we have to come into close contact with him or her. If we wait until we get the big numbers, we will lose ourselves in the numbers and will never be able to show this love and respect for the person." Agitating for fundamental social and political changes might very well be someone else's divine calling, she said, but it was not hers. "Begin in a small way," she told her Sisters and volunteers. "Don't look for numbers. Every small act of love for the unwanted and the poor is important to Jesus."[**]

---

[*]Eileen Egan, *Such a Vision of the Street: Mother Teresa—The Spirit and the Work.* Garden City, NY: Doubleday, 1985, p. 344.

[**]Christian Feldman, *Mother Teresa: Love Stays.* New York: Crossroad Publishing, 1998, pp. 129-130; Kathyrn Spink, *Mother Teresa: A Complete Authorized Biography.* San Francisco: HarperCollins, 1997, p. 88.

Norwegian press was overwhelmingly positive in their assessment of the celebrated champion of the world's destitute and forgotten. "How good it is to experience the world press for once spellbound by a real star, with a real glitter, a star without a sign, without a painted face, without false eyelashes, without a mink and without diamonds, without the theatrical gestures and airs," wrote one Norwegian journalist. "Her only thought is how to use the Nobel Prize in the best possible way, for the world's poorest of the poor."[49]

CHAPTER 6

"A Pencil in God's Hand"

T hree months after receiving the Nobel Peace Prize, Mother Teresa was awarded India's ultimate civilian honor, the *Bharat Ratna,* or "Jewel of India." Bestowed for the highest degrees of service to the country, the Bharat Ratna was established in 1954. More than a quarter of a century later, Mother Teresa became the first recipient of the award who had not been born in India. During the presentation ceremony, India's president, Neelam Sanjiva Reddy, said of Mother Teresa: "She embodies in herself compassion and love of humanity as few in history have done. . . . Her entire life has been a personification of service and compassion. These are the imperatives of human existence which are generally affirmed in words but denied in actions."[50]

A COURAGEOUS MISSION OF MERCY

Mother Teresa's extraordinary "compassion for and love of humanity" were evident in August 1982, when she risked her own life to save a group of disabled children in war-torn Beirut, Lebanon. For years, Lebanon's capital had been afflicted by sporadic fighting between rival Christian and Muslim militia groups. Taking advantage of the political and social chaos spawned by the ongoing Muslim–Christian violence, the Palestinian Liberation Organization (PLO), a group dedicated to the creation of an independent Palestinian state in Israel, put down deep roots in Lebanon. Soon, the PLO had established a virtual state-within-a-state, with its headquarters in West Beirut. In response to increased terrorist raids on Israel from Lebanese soil, during the summer of 1982, the Israeli army launched a major offensive against PLO bases located on the soil of their northern neighbor. The Israelis also laid siege to Beirut, in hopes of forcing out PLO leader Yasir Arafat and the rest of the organization's leadership.

Since 1979, the Missionaries of Charity had operated a house in predominantly Christian East Beirut. On August 10, 1982, at the height of the Israeli siege of the Lebanese capital, Mother Teresa arrived at the convent, determined to assist her Sisters in sheltering and comforting Beirut's beleaguered civilian population. From the head of the Red Cross delegation in East Beirut, she heard about a group of mentally and physically disabled children in predominantly Muslim West Beirut who desperately needed help. The boys and girls had become stranded in their bomb-damaged asylum and were rapidly running out of food and fresh water. Brushing aside warnings from local church and government authorities, Mother Teresa resolved to cross the "Green Line," the dangerous zone dividing Christian East Beirut from Muslim West Beirut, to evacuate the children.

On August 12, Mother Teresa entered West Beirut in a small convoy of four Red Cross vehicles. At the damaged asylum, she discovered more than 60 terrified and hungry children, many of them with severe physical and mental handicaps. Two days after transporting approximately half of the asylum's young patients to the Missionaries of Charity convent in East Beirut, Mother Teresa made the dangerous journey across the heavily militarized Green Line once again to bring back the remaining children. Impressed by the 72-year-old nun's take-charge attitude as much as her compassion, one Red Cross official in Beirut described Mother Teresa as "a cross between a military commander and St. Francis."[51] (Generally considered one of the greatest of Christian saints, St. Francis of Assisi was famous for his compassionate concern for others.)

THE LEPERS OF THE WEST

Almost exactly one year after her perilous mission of mercy into West Beirut, Mother Teresa suffered a serious heart attack while on a visit to Rome. Despite warnings from her physicians, however, she refused to cut back on her grueling schedule, which included a great deal of international travel to found new houses, check on those already established, and lecture before a variety of religious and charitable organizations.

In 1985, Mother Teresa made the long journey from Calcutta to Washington, D.C., to receive America's highest civilian award, the Presidential Medal of Freedom, from President Ronald Reagan. Immediately following the award ceremony, she headed to nearby George Washington University Hospital to visit with patients suffering from Acquired Immunodeficiency Syndrome, or AIDS, a disease caused by a virus that attacks the body's immune system. Mother Teresa met with the patients at the urging of a local doctor who was dismayed by the extreme prejudice that AIDS sufferers, most of whom were gay men or intravenous drug users, were forced to endure. As a result of her personal encounters with the patients at George Washington Hospital, Mother Teresa became determined to help anguished and shunned AIDS victims, whom she labeled the "new lepers of the West."[52]

On Christmas Eve, 1985, Mother Teresa opened the first of what would be a series of hospices for AIDS sufferers in the United States and Europe, where those in the terminal stages of the disease could spend their last weeks or months in a comfortable, loving environment. The hospices were desperately needed,

Mother Teresa bows toward President Ronald Reagan during the ceremony in which he presented her with the Medal of Freedom on June 21, 1985.

she believed, because far too many AIDS patients were abandoned, even by their own families, and left to face what was usually an agonizingly painful death alone. Named "Gift of Love," the first Missionaries of Charity hospice was located in one of the areas hardest struck by the AIDS epidemic in America: New York City. "We are not here to sit in judgment on these people, to decide blame or guilt," Mother Teresa explained at the opening of the Manhattan hospice. "Our mission is to help them, to make their dying days more tolerable."[53]

MISSION TO EASTERN EUROPE

During the late 1980s and early 1990s, as the totalitarian and often stridently atheistic Communist regimes of Eastern Europe began

Letter to George H.W. Bush and Saddam Hussein

The following is an excerpt from a letter written by Mother Teresa to U.S. President George Herbert Walker Bush and Iraqi President Saddam Hussein on January 2, 1991, at the beginning of the Persian Gulf War between their two nations.

Dear President George Bush and President Saddam Hussein:

I come to you with tears in my eyes and God's love in my heart to plead to you for the poor and those who will become poor if the war that we all dread and fear happens. I beg you with my whole heart to work for, to labor for God's peace and to be reconciled with one another.

You both have your cases to make and your people to care for but first please listen to the One who came into the world to teach us peace. You have the power and the strength to destroy God's presence and image, His men, His women, and His children. Please listen to the will of God. God has created us to be loved by His love and not be destroyed by our hatred.

In the short term there may be winners and losers in this war that we all dread but that never can nor never will justify the suffering, pain and loss of life which your weapons will cause. I come to you in the name of God, the God that we all love and share, to beg for the innocent ones, our poor of the world and those who will become poor because of war. They are the ones who will suffer most because they have no means of escape. I plead on bended knee for them. They will suffer and when they do we will be the ones who are guilty for not having done all

to weaken and crumble, Mother Teresa decided to focus much of her energy on opening missions in a part of the world that had long been closed to her order. In 1987, the Soviet government allowed Mother Teresa into the USSR for the first time ever, so that she could meet with the survivors of the devastating nuclear power plant accident at Chernobyl. By the early 1990s, the Missionaries of Charity had established houses in the Soviet Union, Hungary,

in our power to protect and love them. I plead to you for those who will be left orphaned, widowed, and left alone because their parents, husbands, brothers and children have been killed. *I beg you please save them.* I plead for those who will be left with disability and disfigurement. They are God's children. I please for those who will be left with no home, no food and no love. Please think of them as being your children. Finally I plead for those who will have the most precious thing that God can give us, Life, taken away from them. I beg you to save our brothers and sisters, yours and ours, because they are given to us by God to love and to cherish. It is not for us to destroy what God has given us. Please, please let your mind and your will become the mind and will of God. You have the power to bring war into the world or to build peace. PLEASE CHOOSE THE WAY OF PEACE.

I, my sisters and our poor are praying for you so much. The whole world is praying that you will open your hearts in love to God. You may win the war but what will the cost be on people who are broken, disabled and lost?

I appeal to you—to your love, your love of God and your fellowmen. In the name of God and in the name of those you will make poor do not destroy life and peace. Let the love and peace triumph and let your name be remembered for the good you have done, the joy you have spread and the love you have shared.*

---

*Paul Williams, *The Life and Work of Mother Teresa*. Indianapolis: Alpha, 2002, pp. 215–216.

Czechoslovakia, and Romania, where they focused on helping the thousands of abandoned, orphaned, and disabled children forced to live under appalling conditions in state-run asylums during the regime of fallen Communist dictator Nicolae Ceauşescu.

In 1991, Mother Teresa realized a long-standing dream, when she opened a Missionaries of Charity house in Tirana, Albania, just as the country's oppressive Marxist regime was beginning to falter following the death of longtime dictator Enver Hoxha. Albania held a special place in Mother Teresa's heart, not only because it was the land of her ancestors but also because it was the poorest country in all Europe. Soon, she had founded two additional homes for the destitute in Tirana and Shkoder, and convinced Albania's president to reopen several Catholic churches that had been taken over by the government years earlier. A firm believer in religious tolerance, Mother Teresa insisted that the government permit Albania's Muslim majority to reopen a number of mosques that had been shut down by the repressive Hoxha regime, as well.

FAMOUS FRIENDS AND ADMIRERS

While Mother Teresa was crisscrossing the globe on her various missions of mercy during the 1980s and early 1990s, she was also developing close friendships with two of the most beloved figures of the late twentieth century: Pope John Paul II and Princess Diana of Great Britain. Mother Teresa and Pope John Paul II met for the first time not long after the charismatic Polish cleric was elected pope in October 1978. They quickly discovered that they had much in common. Both had been brought up in Eastern Europe, both had lost a beloved parent as a child, and both were staunch supporters of traditional Catholic doctrine and practice, and particularly the Church's longstanding prohibitions against abortion, artificial contraception, and female priests.

In 1986, the warm personal relationship that had developed between Pope John Paul II and Mother Teresa became evident to the world, when the pope made a point of visiting the Missionaries of Charity mother house and Nirmal Hriday during an official trip to India. After embracing the diminutive nun and placing a garland that had originally been meant for him around her neck, Pope John Paul prayed in the mother house chapel before setting off for Mother Teresa's home for the dying at Kalighat. For nearly an hour, he toured Nirmal Hriday with Mother Teresa, blessing the dying men and women and even helping to feed those residents who could still eat. Paying tribute to Mother Teresa's tireless work for society's unwanted and forgotten, the pope said: "For the destitute and dying, Nirmal Hriday is a place of hope. This place represents the profound dignity of every human person."[54] Mother Teresa, in her turn, was thrilled by the pontiff's visit, later describing it as "the happiest day of her life," according to her friend and biographer, Kathryn Spink.[55]

More than a decade after she first met Pope John Paul II, Mother Teresa made friends with another of the most popular international celebrities of the era, Princess Diana of Great Britain. The attractive and fashionable young princess had been the darling of the international press ever since her wedding to Prince Charles, the heir to the British throne, in July 1981. Diana was widely admired by the press and public alike, not only for her beauty and sense of style but also for her devotion to a variety of charitable causes.

When Diana and Mother Teresa were both invited to speak at the International Congress for the Family in London in 1989, Mother Teresa was delighted to have the opportunity to meet the philanthropic princess. She announced:

> I am coming to Britain to meet Princess Diana. I do not really have the time but I must be there. . . . Everywhere there is a need for giving and Diana has more influence over the British people than anybody else. If she tells them how important it is to make their families strong they will listen, if she asks them

Mother Teresa walks with Princess Diana after receiving a visit from her on June 18, 1997, in New York. The two women first met in 1992, when Princess Diana made a special stop to meet Mother Teresa in the Roman hospital where she was recuperating following a bout of illness.

to care for the poor, for the homeless, they will hear her. So I must speak to her while I have the chance.[56]

As it turned out, a scheduling mix-up prevented Diana and Mother Teresa from meeting in London in 1989. Nearly three years later, in September 1992, Diana toured Nirmal Hriday during a state visit to India and greatly impressed the staff by her willingness "to touch the suffering bodies of India's most rejected," noted Spink.[57] To both Mother Teresa and Diana's immense disappointment, however, the increasingly frail nun had fallen ill on a recent trip to the Vatican and was stuck in a Roman hospital during the entire royal visit to India. On the spur of the moment, though, the princess decided to make a stopover in Rome on her way home from Calcutta, so that she could speak with Mother Teresa in person at last. By all accounts, there was an instant rapport between the two women.

Over the next several years, Mother Teresa and Princess Diana remained in close contact. When Diana's marriage to Charles ended in 1996, Mother Teresa told an interviewer that she loved the 35-year-old princess as a daughter. Although she had consistently backed the official Church stance against divorce in the past, Mother Teresa was prepared to make an exception in Diana's case. When asked for her reaction to the royal breakup, she mused: "I think it is a sad story. Diana is such a sad soul. She gives so much love but she needs to get it back. You know what? It is good that it is over. Nobody was happy anyhow."[58]

CONTROVERSY

By the 1990s, Mother Teresa's expanding network of missions around the globe, as well as her very public friendships with two widely admired celebrities, Pope Paul John II and Princess Diana, had garnered the tiny nun more positive publicity than ever before. Indeed, many people were starting to refer to Mother Teresa as nothing less than a living saint. Nonetheless, during the

Pope John Paul II is shown here with Mother Teresa, during an official visit to Calcutta in 1986. The pope toured Nirmal Hriday with Mother Teresa, on a day that the nun later described as the happiest of her life.

early and mid-1990s, the Missionaries of Charity and its founder were plagued by controversy.

Mother Teresa's problems began in May 1993, when she shocked the membership of the International Association of Co-Workers by suddenly disbanding the lay organization founded 25 years earlier by Ann Blaikie. Although the association's officials had repeatedly assured Mother Teresa that all money donated to the group went directly to the poor, she had become convinced that funds earmarked for the destitute were actually being spent on printing organizational newsletters or sending members to international conferences. She also felt that the association had become top-heavy with administrators and had lost its original simplicity.

The organization had played a vital role over the years in supporting the Missionaries of Charity, through the labor of its members and through the large sums of money they raised for the order. Consequently, tens of thousands of International Association of Co-Workers members were both puzzled and bitterly disappointed when Mother Teresa announced her intention to dissolve their organization. Three years after her stunning move, wrote Anne Sebba, Mother Teresa "was still having to write letters to her Co-Workers asking them 'to pray for the few who still find it difficult to accept my decision because they do not as yet see it as the will of God for the Co-Workers.'"[59]

A year and a half after Mother Teresa disbanded the International Association of Co-Workers, she found herself in the midst of another controversy. This one centered on a 30-minute film about Mother Teresa entitled *Hell's Angel*, which aired on British television in November 1994. Written and narrated by journalist Christopher Hitchens, the program accused Mother Teresa of accepting money for her work from corrupt dictators, such as Haiti's notorious former leader, Jean-Claude "Baby Doc" Duvalier. In addition, Hitchens blasted Mother Teresa for condemning all use of contraceptives, despite the Third World's soaring population, and for providing substandard medical care to patients in her homes for the dying.

Public response to the program was swift and angry. Most viewers were outraged by what they considered an unfair and biased attack on a woman who had accomplished so much good in the world. They condemned the film as offensive, sensationalist, and misleading. Nonetheless, there were those in the public and the press who commended Hitchens for at least having the nerve to open a discussion regarding someone who had previously been considered to be untouchable. As for Mother Teresa, she told an interviewer shortly after the derogatory program was aired that she had not seen the film herself but that she "forgave" Hitchens and the documentary's producer for making it.[60]

STEPPING DOWN

During the 1990s, Mother Teresa was beset not only by controversy but also by a series of grave health problems. In November 1996, after suffering a near-fatal heart attack, she informed her Sisters that she could no longer continue as Superior General of the Missionaries of Charity. Choosing a replacement for their dynamic and beloved founder proved a lengthy and difficult process for the 123 delegates from around the globe. Nonetheless, they gathered in Calcutta during the winter of 1997 to elect Mother Teresa's successor.

In March, the Sisters finally announced that 63-year-old Sister Nirmala, a native of Nepal, would be their new Superior General. Nirmala had converted from Hinduism to Christianity soon after graduating from a Catholic convent school at age 17. The highly educated and deeply spiritual nun was one of the Missionaries of Charity's earliest and most devoted members, and Mother Teresa was clearly pleased with the delegates' selection.

On August 26, 1997, Mother Teresa, by now almost entirely bedridden, observed her eighty-seventh birthday in the mother house in Calcutta. Not quite a week later, the untimely death of Princess Diana in an automobile accident prompted Mother Teresa to make what was to be her final public statement. Lauding the 36-year-old princess's dedication to the world's poor and unwanted, Mother Teresa pledged that she and her Sisters of Charity would offer up special prayers for Diana's soul.

"THE ONLY THING THAT COUNTS"

On Friday, September 5, 1997, the same day that Princess Diana's funeral was held in London, Mother Teresa died in the Calcutta convent that had been her home for 47 years. Shortly after fin-

Sister Nirmala (right), one of the earliest members of the Missionaries of Charity, was elected to be Mother Teresa's successor in 1997. The two nuns are shown in a photograph from March 1997, shortly after Sister Nirmala was declared the new Superior General.

ishing evening prayers, she complained of a searing pain in her spine. "I cannot breathe," she reportedly told her physician.[61] Minutes later, Mother Teresa's heart stopped beating.

As news of Mother Teresa's death spread throughout the world, religious and secular leaders rushed to pay tribute. In Rome, Pope John Paul II was "deeply moved and pained" by Mother Teresa's death, a Vatican spokesman reported, "because he was very close to this sister who dedicated her life to helping people in the world who were the poorest, the most neglected and the abandoned."[62] In Washington, D.C., the U.S. Congress, which only a few months earlier had granted her its prestigious Gold Medal, observed a moment of silence in Mother Teresa's honor. In Oslo, Norway, Francis Sejersted, the chair of the Norwegian Nobel Committee, noted that the woman whom the Indians called "the Saint of the Gutters" had become a powerful symbol

Legacy of the Peacemaker

Today, nearly a decade after Mother Teresa's death, her remarkable spirit of compassion and faith live on. Even as other Catholic religious orders struggle to bring in new members, the order that Mother Teresa founded in 1950 continues to attract novices from all over the globe. As of the early twenty-first century, about 5,000 Missionaries of Charity nuns and 450 brothers operated nearly 600 missions in 120 countries. Supported entirely by private donations, these missions include leprosy, AIDS, alcohol, and drug treatment centers; homes for the dying; orphanages; schools; and shelters for the homeless and battered women.

Mother Teresa's selfless example of giving also continues to inspire thousands of volunteers—Catholic and non-Catholic alike—to donate their time and talents to assist the Missionaries of Charity. As during her lifetime, Mother Teresa remains a powerful symbol of love, hope, and peace for people of all backgrounds. According to religious scholar and journalist Kenneth L. Woodward:

> Although [Mother Teresa] was a Roman Catholic, her simplicity and manifest concern for the dying, the abandoned and the outcast transcended boundaries of religion and nationality. "By blood and origin I am Albanian," she once said of herself. "My citizenship is Indian. I am a Catholic nun. As to my calling, I belong to the world. As to my heart, I belong entirely to the heart of Jesus."*

For the world's estimated one billion Roman Catholics, Mother Teresa's legacy is also a profoundly spiritual one. During the last years of her life, many people referred to the diminutive nun as a living saint. Six years after her death, Teresa's loyal friend and supporter Pope John Paul II presided over her beatification, the final step before sainthood or canonization in the Catholic Church. On October 19, 2003, more than 300,000 people jammed into St. Peter's Square in Vatican City to witness the beatification of the woman who would henceforth be known as Blessed Mother Teresa of Kolkata and could now be publicly venerated (honored). (The city of Calcutta was officially renamed Kolkata in 2001 by the government of West Bengal.)

Although there is traditionally a five-year waiting period before a deceased individual can be nominated for beatification within the Catholic Church, Pope John Paul so admired Mother Teresa that he put forth her name for that honor in 1999, just two years after the nun's death. For the next five years, Vatican officials scrutinized Mother Teresa's life, writings, and work, and interviewed her supporters and her critics, to determine if she was worthy of the title Blessed Mother Teresa. These interviews were used to determine whether she had consistently exhibited the core virtues of a saint: faith, charity, hope, justice, humility, sound judgment, moral strength, and temperance.

The Vatican researchers also sought proof of one posthumous miracle, a necessary prerequisite for beatification. Since her death, many people had contacted the Catholic Church, claiming to have been miraculously healed after praying to Mother Teresa. After the Vatican reviewed all the petitions, it chose to officially recognize as a miracle the claim of an impoverished Bengali woman named Monica Besra. Besra's large stomach tumor had allegedly disappeared in 1998 five hours after several Missionaries of Charity Sisters prayed to Mother Teresa for a cure and held a medallion with the dead nun's image to the Hindu woman's abdomen. (According to Besra's physician, however, the prescription drugs that he administered to the 35-year-old mother of five were actually responsible for the disappearance of her tumor.)

Before Mother Teresa can officially be declared a saint, a second "divine sign"—again in the form of a posthumous miracle—must be verified by the Vatican. As Kenneth Woodward noted shortly after Mother Teresa's beatification in 2003, however, "For most Catholics she is already worthy of being called a saint."**

*Kenneth L. Woodward, "Little Sister of the Poor," *Newsweek*, September 15, 1997, p. 70.

**Kenneth L. Woodward, "The Fast Track to Sainthood: How This Diminutive Nun Got Beatified a Record Seven Years After Her Death," *Newsweek*, October 20, 2003, p. 52.

of humanitarianism: "Hers is one of the awards we look back on with great joy and satisfaction," he declared.[63]

The Indian government and people felt a profound respect and gratitude for the Nobel Peace laureate and nearly seven-decade-long resident of their nation. So, on Saturday, September 13, Mother Teresa was honored with an Indian state funeral. The same army gun carriage on which the bodies of modern India's two greatest heroes—Mohandas Gandhi and India's first prime minister, Jawaharlal Nehru—had once rested, carried Mother Teresa's coffin through the crowd-lined streets of Calcutta. At the city's giant Netaji Indoor Stadium, about 15,000 people, including presidents, prime ministers, first ladies, queens, and other dignitaries from around the world, attended a three-hour funeral service for the devout nun. Conducted in three different languages—English, Hindi, and Bengali—the service included a Roman Catholic Mass as well as special blessings over the coffin by representatives from India's major faiths, including Hinduism, Islam, and Buddhism. After the service, Indian troops conveyed Mother Teresa's body back to the mother house, where she was buried beneath a plain stone slab. "Her gravestone bears no name," wrote biographer Paul Williams, "only this simple inscription from the Gospel of John: 'Love one another as I have loved you.'"[64]

At the time of Mother Teresa's death, the Missionaries of Charity included about 4,000 Sisters and 569 centers in more than 100 different countries. All were committed to serving the destitute, the ill, and the unwanted. Despite her remarkable achievements and the many prestigious honors she received during her lifetime, however, Mother Teresa always saw herself as no more than a willing servant of Heaven, "a little pencil" in God's hand, as she put it.[65] She once said,

> God works in his own way in the hearts of human beings, and
> we can't know how close they are to him. But we will always
> know from their actions whether they are at his disposal or not.
> Whether Hindu, Muslim, or Christian, how you live your life

St. Peter's Square in Vatican City is shown here during the beatification ceremony of Mother Teresa led by Pope John Paul II in October 2003. After the ceremony, Mother Teresa would be known as the Blessed Mother Teresa of Kolkata, one step away from sainthood.

proves whether or not you belong completely to him. . . . We may not judge or condemn. . . . The only thing that counts is that we love.[66]

With unfailing humility and boundless charity, Mother Teresa put her love of God and her fellow humans into action, providing food to the hungry, shelter to the homeless, and comfort to the dying. In the process, she became one of the most celebrated and admired Nobel Peace Prize laureates—and individuals—of the twentieth century.

APPENDIX

Nobel Peace Prize Lecture of Mother Teresa

Let us thank God for the opportunity that we all have together today, for this gift of peace that reminds us that we have been created to live that peace, and Jesus became man to bring that good news to the poor. . . .

[Jesus Christ] was . . . the first messenger of peace. . . . He died on the cross to show that greater love, and he died for you and for me and for that leper and for that man dying of hunger and that naked person lying in the street not only of Calcutta, but of Africa, and New York, and London, and Oslo—and insisted that we love one another as he loves each one of us. And we read that in the Gospel very clearly—love as I have loved you—as I love you—as the Father has loved me, I love you—and the harder the Father loved him, he gave him to us, and how much we love one another, we, too, must give to each other until it hurts. It is not enough for us to say: I love God, but I do not love my neighbor. St. John says you are a liar if you say you love God and you don't love your neighbor. How can you love God whom you do not see, if you do not love your neighbor whom you see, whom you touch, with whom you live. And so this is very important for us to realize that love, to be true, has to hurt. It hurt Jesus to love us, it hurt him. . . . We have been created in his image. We have been created to love and be loved. . . . He makes himself the hungry one—the naked one—the homeless one—the sick one—the one in prison—the lonely one—the unwanted one—and he says: You did it to me. Hungry for our love, and this is the hunger of our poor people. This is the hunger that you and I must find, it may be in our own home.

I never forget an opportunity I had in visiting a home where they had all these old parents of sons and daughters who had just put them in an institution and forgotten maybe. And I went there, and I saw in that home they had everything, beautiful things, but everybody was looking towards the door. And I did not see a single one with their smile on their face. And I turned to the Sister and I asked: How is that? How is it that the people they have everything here, why are they all looking towards the door, why are they not smiling? I am so used to see the smile on our people, even the dying one smile, and she said: This is nearly every day, they are expecting, they are hoping that a son or daughter will come to visit them. They are hurt because they are forgotten, and see—this is where love comes. That poverty comes right there in our own home, even neglect to love. Maybe in our own family we have somebody who is feeling lonely, who is feeling sick, who is feeling worried, and these are difficult days for everybody. Are we there, are we there to receive them, is the mother there to receive the child?

I was surprised in the West to see so many young boys and girls given into drugs, and I tried to find out why—why is it like that, and the answer was: Because there is no one in the family to receive them. Father and mother are so busy they have no time. Young parents are in some institution and the child takes back to the street and gets involved in something. We are talking of peace. These are things that break peace, but I feel the greatest destroyer of peace today is abortion, because it is a direct war, a direct killing—direct murder by the mother herself. And we read in the Scripture, for God says very clearly: Even if a mother could forget her child—I will not forget you—I have carved you in the palm of my hand. We are carved in the palm of His hand, so close to Him that unborn child has been carved in the hand of God. And that is what strikes me most, the beginning of that sentence, that even if a mother could forget something impossible—but even if she could forget—I will not forget you. And today the greatest means—the greatest destroyer of peace is abortion. And we who are standing here—our parents wanted us. We would not be here if our parents would do that to us. . . . Many people are very, very concerned with the children in India, with the children in Africa where quite a number die, maybe of malnutrition, of hunger and so on, but millions are dying deliberately by the will of the mother. And this is what is the greatest destroyer of peace today. Because if a mother can kill her own child—what is left for me to kill you and you kill me—there is nothing between. And this I appeal in India, I appeal everywhere: Let us bring the child back, and this year being the child's year: What have we done for the child? . . . Let us make this year that we make every single child born, and unborn, wanted. And today is the end of the year, have we really made the children wanted? I will give you something terrifying. We are fighting abortion by adoption, we have saved thousands of lives, we have sent words to all the clinics, to the hospitals, police stations—please don't destroy the child, we will take the child. So every hour of the day and night it is always somebody, we have quite a number of unwedded mothers—tell them come, we will take care of you, we will take the child from you, and we will get a home for the child. And we have a tremendous demand from families who have no children, that is the blessing of God for us. And also, we are doing another thing which is very beautiful—we are teaching our beggars, our leprosy patients, our slum dwellers, our people of the street, natural family planning. . . .

The poor people are very great people. They can teach us so many beautiful things. The other day one of them came to thank me and said: You people who have vowed chastity you are the best people to teach us family planning. Because it is nothing more than self-control out of love for each other. And I think they said a beautiful sentence. And these are people who maybe have nothing to eat, maybe they have not a home where to live, but they are great people. The poor are very wonderful people. One evening we went out and we picked up four people from the street. And one of them was in a most terrible condition—and I told the Sisters: You take care of the other three, I take care of this one that looked worse. So I did for her all that my love can do. I put her in bed, and there was such a beautiful smile on her face. She took hold of my hand, as she said one word only: Thank you—and she died.

I could not help but examine my conscience before her, and I asked what would I say if I was in her place. And my answer was very simple. I would have tried to draw a little attention to myself, I would have said I am hungry, that I am dying, I am cold, I am in pain, or something, but she gave me much more—she gave me her grateful love. And she died with a smile on her face. As that man whom we picked up from the drain, half eaten with worms, and we brought him to the home. I have lived like an animal in the street, but I am going to die like an angel, loved and cared for. And it was so wonderful to see the greatness of that man who could speak like that, who could die like that without blaming anybody, without cursing anybody, without comparing anything. Like an angel—this is the greatness of our people. And that is why we believe what Jesus had said: I was hungry—I was naked—I was homeless—I was unwanted, unloved, uncared for—and you did it to me.

I believe that we are not real social workers. We may be doing social work in the eyes of the people, but we are really contemplatives in the heart of the world. For we are touching the Body of Christ 24 hours. We have 24 hours in this presence, and so you and I. You too try to bring that presence of God in your family, for the family that prays together stays together. And I think that we in our family don't need bombs and guns, to destroy to bring peace—just get together, love one another, bring that peace, that joy, that strength of presence of each other in the home. And we will be able to overcome all the evil that is in the world.

There is so much suffering, so much hatred, so much misery, and we with our prayer, with our sacrifice are beginning at home. Love begins at home, and it is not how much we do, but how much love we put in the action that we do. It is to God Almighty—how much we do it does not matter, because He is infinite, but how much love we put in that action. How much we do to Him in the person that we are serving. . . .

And with this prize that I have received as a prize of peace, I am going to try to make the home for many people that have no home. Because I believe that love begins at home, and if we can create a home for the poor—I think that more and more love will spread. And we will be able through this understanding love to bring peace, bring the good news to the poor. The poor in our own family first, in our country and in the world. . . .

I never forget some time ago about fourteen professors came from the United States from different universities. And they came to Calcutta to our house. Then we were talking about that they had been to the home for the dying. We have a home for the dying in Calcutta, where we have picked up more than 36,000 people only from the streets of Calcutta, and out of that big number more than 18,000 have died a beautiful death. They have just gone home to God; and they came to our house and we talked of love, of compassion, and then one of them asked me: Say, Mother, please tell us something that we will remember, and I said to them: Smile at each other, make time for each other in your family. Smile at each other. . . . If we could only remember that God loves me, and I have an opportunity to love others as he loves me, not in big things, but in small things with great love, then Norway becomes a nest of love. And how beautiful it will be that from here a center for peace has been given. That from here the joy of life of the unborn child comes out. If you become a burning light in the world of peace, then really the Nobel Peace Prize is a gift of the Norwegian people. God bless you!

Source: Mother Teresa, Nobel Lecture. Available at http://nobleprize.org/ nobel_prizes/peace/laureates/1979/teresa-lecture.html. © 1979 The Nobel Foundation.

CHRONOLOGY

1910	**August 26.** Mother Teresa is born in Skopje, Macedonia, as Agnes Gonxha Bojaxhiu.
1919	Her father, Nikola Bojaxhiu, dies under mysterious circumstances.
1928	Agnes joins Irish branch of the Institute of the Blessed Virgin Mary, the Sisters of Loreto.
1929	She begins her novitiate in Darjeeling, India.
1931	As Sister Teresa, she starts teaching at a girls' school in Calcutta, India, operated by the Loreto Sisters.
1937	Sister Teresa takes her final vows as a Loreto Sister. She is now known as Mother Teresa.
1939–1945	Europe is embroiled in World War II.
1946	Mother Teresa receives the call to serve God among "the poorest of the poor" while on a train journey.
1947	India achieves independence from British rule.
1948	Mother Teresa moves to the slums of Calcutta and opens her first school there.
1950	The Vatican officially approves her new religious order, the Missionaries of Charity.
1952	Nirmal Hriday, her first home for the dying and destitute, opens in Calcutta.
1953	Shishu Bhavan, a home for abandoned and orphaned children, opens.

1957 Missionaries of Charity begin ministering to lepers in Calcutta.

1965 Missionaries of Charity is declared a pontifical order and can now expand its work beyond India.

1969 British documentary *Something Beautiful for God* brings Mother Teresa international attention.

1979 Mother Teresa wins the Nobel Peace Prize.

1980 She is awarded the "Jewel of India" (Bharat Ratna) award.

1985 She is awarded the U.S. Presidential Medal of Freedom.

1994 "Hell's Angel," a highly critical television documentary on Mother Teresa, airs in Great Britain.

1997 **September 5.** Mother Teresa dies in Calcutta at age 87.

2003 Mother Teresa is beatified by Pope John Paul II.

NOTES

Chapter 2

1. Quoted in Anne Sebba, *Mother Teresa: Beyond the Image*. New York: Doubleday, 1997, p. 5.
2. Quoted in Eileen Egan, *Such a Vision of the Street: Mother Teresa—The Spirit and the Work*. Garden City, N.Y.: Doubleday, 1985, p. 8.
3. Quoted in David Porter, *Mother Teresa: The Early Years*. Grand Rapids, Mich.: W.B. Eerdmans, 1986, p. 20.
4. Quoted in Kathyrn Spink, *Mother Teresa: A Complete Authorized Biography*. San Francisco: HarperCollins, 1997, p. 6.
5. Quoted in Porter, *Mother Teresa,* p. 13.
6. Quoted in Spink, *Mother Teresa*, pp. 6–7.
7. Quoted in Christian Feldman, *Mother Teresa: Love Stays*. New York: Crossroad Publishing, 1998, p. 16.
8. Ibid., p. 13.
9. Egan, *Such a Vision of the Street,* p. 11.
10. Quoted in Navin Chawla, *Mother Teresa: The Authorized Biography*. Rockport, Mass.: Element, 1992, p. 4.
11. Quoted in Malcolm Muggeridge, *Something Beautiful for God.* San Francisco: Harper & Row, 1971, p. 84.
12. Quoted in Sebba, *Mother Teresa*, p. 19.
13. Quoted in Chawla, *Mother Teresa*, pp. 1–2.
14. Spink, *Mother Teresa*, pp. 10–11.
15. Quoted in Chawla, *Mother Teresa*, p. 5.

Chapter 3

16. Quoted in David Scott, *A Revolution of Love: The Meaning of Mother Teresa*. Chicago: Loyola Press, p. 43.
17. Quoted in Porter, *Mother Teresa*, pp. 35–36.
18. Ibid., p. 37.
19. Ibid., pp. 40–42.
20. Quoted in Spink, *Mother Teresa*, p. 19.
21. Sebba, *Mother Teresa*, p. 44.
22. Quoted in Sebba, *Mother Teresa*, p. 44.
23. Quoted in Egan, *Such a Vision of the Streets*, p. 24.

Chapter 4

24. Quoted in Scott, *A Revolution of Love*, p. 74.
25. Quoted in Paul Williams, *The Life and Work of Mother Teresa*. Indianapolis: Alpha, 2002, p. 43.
26. Quoted in Williams, *The Life and Work of Mother Teresa*, p. 43.
27. Egan, *Such a Vision of the Streets*, p. 27.
28. Quoted in Egan, *Such a Vision of the Streets*, p. 29.
29. Sebba, *Mother Teresa,* p. 49.
30. Williams, *The Life and Work of Mother Teresa*, p. 50.
31. Quoted in Mother Teresa, *Essential Writings*. Maryknoll, N.Y.: Orbis, 2001, p. 38.

32. Chawla, *Mother Teresa*, p. xv.
33. Quoted in Egan, *Such A Vision of the Streets*, p. 60.
34. Quoted in Sebba, *Mother Teresa*, p. 58.
35. Quoted in Feldman, *Mother Teresa*, p. 47.
36. Ibid., p. 46.
37. Quoted in Desmond Doig, *Mother Teresa: Her People and Her Work*. San Francisco: Harper & Row, 1976, p. 169.

Chapter 5

38. Quoted in Spink, *Mother Teresa*, p. 86.
39. Spink, *Mother Teresa*, p. 86.
40. Quoted in Egan, *Such a Vision of the Street*, p. 240.
41. Muggeridge, *Something Beautiful for God*, p. 146.
42. Quoted in Williams, *The Life and Work of Mother Teresa*, p. 133.
43. Quoted in Egan, *Such a Vision of the Street*, p. 347.
44. Quoted in Williams, *The Life and Work of Mother Teresa*, pp. 134–135.
45. Ibid., p. 135.
46. Quoted in Egan, *Such a Vision of the Street*, p. 348.
47. Ibid., p. 349–351.
48. Sebba, *Mother Teresa*, p. 102.
49. Quoted in Williams, *The Life and Work of Mother Teresa*, p. 137.

Chapter 6

50. Quoted in Egan, *Such a Vision of the Street*, p. 357.
51. Ibid., p. 395.
52. Quoted in Sebba, *Mother Teresa*, p. 113.
53. Quoted in Spink, *Mother Teresa*, p. 205.
54. Ibid., p. 178.
55. Spink, *Mother Teresa*, p. 178.
56. Quoted in Sebba, *Mother Teresa*, p. 245.
57. Quoted in Spink, *Mother Teresa*, p. 263.
58. Quoted in Sebba, *Mother Teresa*, p. 245.
59. Sebba, *Mother Teresa*, p. 107.
60. Quoted in Christopher Hitchens, *The Missionary Position: Mother Teresa in Theory and Practice*. London: Verso, 1995, p. 88.
61. Quoted in Kenneth L. Woodward, "Little Sister of the Poor," *Newsweek*, September 15, 1997, p. 70.
62. Quoted in Susan Crimp, *Personal Encounters with Mother Teresa: Touched by a Saint*. Notre Dame: Sorin, 2000, p. 33.
63. Ibid., p. 33.
64. Quoted in Williams, *The Life and Work of Mother Teresa*, p. 5.
65. Quoted in Scott, *A Revolution of Love*, p. 37.
66. Quoted in Feldman, Mother Teresa, pp. 46–47.

BIBLIOGRAPHY

Books

Chawla, Navin. *Mother Teresa: The Authorized Biography.* Rockport, Mass.: Element, 1992.

Crimp, Susan. *Personal Encounters With Mother Teresa: Touched by a Saint.* Notre Dame, Ind.: Sorin, 2000.

Doig, Desmond. *Mother Teresa: Her People and Her Work.* San Francisco: Harper & Row, 1976.

Egan, Eileen. *Such a Vision of the Street: Mother Teresa—the Spirit and the Work.* New York: Doubleday, 1985.

Feldman, Christian. *Mother Teresa: Love Stays.* New York: Crossroad Publishing, 1998.

Hitchens, Christopher. *The Missionary Position: Mother Teresa in Theory and Practice.* New York: Verso, 1995.

Mother Teresa. *Essential Writings.* Maryknoll, N.Y.: Orbis, 2001.

———. *Mother Teresa: In My Own Words.* Compiled by José Louis Ganzález-Balado. Liguori, Mo.: Liguori Publications, 1989.

Muggeridge, Malcolm. *Something Beautiful for God.* San Francisco: Harper & Row, 1971.

Porter, David. *Mother Teresa: The Early Years.* Grand Rapids, Mich.: W.B. Eerdmans, 1986.

Scott, David. *A Revolution of Love: The Meaning of Mother Teresa.* Chicago: Loyola Press, 2005.

Sebba, Anne. *Mother Teresa: Beyond the Image.* New York: Doubleday, 1997.

Spink, Kathyrn. *Mother Teresa: A Complete Authorized Biography.* San Francisco: HarperCollins, 1997.

Williams, Paul. *The Life and Work of Mother Teresa.* Indianapolis: Alpha, 2002.

Articles

Mukherjee, Bharati. "The Saint: Mother Teresa." *Time* (June 14, 1999): p. 88.

Poplin, Mary. "No Humanitarian: A Portrait of Mother Teresa." *Commonweal* (December 19, 1997): pp. 11–14.

Tucker, Ruth A. "Mother Teresa." *Christian History* (February 2000): pp. 20–21.

Woodward, Kenneth L. "The Fast Track to Sainthood: How This Diminutive Nun Got Beatified a Record Seven Years After Her Death." *Newsweek* (October 20, 2003): p. 52.

———. "Little Sister of the Poor." *Newsweek* (September 15, 1997): pp. 70–74.

FURTHER READING

Dils, Tracey E. *Mother Teresa*. Philadelphia: Chelsea House, 2001.

Greene, Meg. *Mother Teresa: A Biography*. Westport, Conn.: Greenwood Press, 2004.

Royle, Roger, and Gary Woods. *Mother Teresa: A Life in Pictures*. San Francisco: HarperCollins, 1992.

Schaefer, Linda. *Come and See: A Photojournalist's Journey into the World of Mother Teresa*. Sanford, Fla.: DC Press, 2003.

Tilton, Rafael. *Mother Teresa*. San Diego: Lucent, 2000.

Web sites

Gjoni, Landi. Mother Teresa: 1910–1997.
http://www.drini.com/motherteresa/index2.html

"Mother Teresa: 1979 Nobel Peace Prize Laureate," Nobel Prize Internet Archive.
http://almaz.com/nobel/peace/1979a.html

"Mother Teresa—Nobel Lecture," Nobelprize.org.
http://nobelprize.org/peace/laureates/1979/teresa-lecture.html

Mother Teresa of Calcutta Center.
http://www.motherteresa.org/layout.html

PICTURE CREDITS

INDEX

LOUISE CHIPLEY SLAVICEK received her master's degree in history from the University of Connecticut. She is the author of 15 other books for young people, including *Women of the American Revolution, Israel, The Great Wall of China, Mao Zedong,* and *Carlos Santana.* She lives in Ohio with her husband, Jim, a research biologist, and their two children, Krista and Nathan.